D. L. MOODY

The American Evangelist

Bonnie C. Harvey

BARBOUR
PUBLISHING, INC.
Uhrichsville, Ohio

Other books in the "Heroes of the Faith" series:

John Bunyan
William Carey
Fanny Crosby
Jim Elliot
Billy Graham
David Livingstone
John Newton
Gladys Aylward
Samuel Morris
Charles Spurgeon
Corrie ten Boom
Mother Teresa
Sojourner Truth
John Wesley
Mary Slessor
George Müller
C. S. Lewis
Watchman Nee
Martin Luther
George Washington Carver
Amy Carmichael

© MCMXCVII by Barbour Publishing, Inc.

ISBN 1-55748-932-7

Published by Barbour Publishing, Inc., P.O. Box 719, Uhrichsville, OH 44683
http://www.barbourbooks.com

ecpa Member of the
Evangelical Christian
Publishers Association

Printed in the United States of America.

D. L. MOODY

To Ray—posthumously: With deep love and affection for helping me to appreciate D. L. Moody, his person, and his ministry.

one

"The world has yet to see what God will do with a man fully consecrated to Him," the English butcher and lay preacher Henry Varley observed to D. L. Moody as they left an all-night prayer meeting. His words stuck with Moody. Having traveled to Britain that summer of 1872, Moody was seeking rest and renewal. Varley's words gave him a new goal.

"A man!" Moody wrote. "Varley meant any man. Varley didn't say he had to be educated or brilliant, or anything else. Just a man. Well, by the Holy Spirit in me, I'll be that man."

Soon after Moody made that vow, a Congregational minister in London invited him to preach at Arundel Square in a lower-middle-class district. Visiting during the Sunday morning sermon, Moody was irritated at the congregation's undifference. The people seemed to be lifeless and disinterested in anything the minister had to say. Moody was tempted not to preach that night and wondered what message he could possibly bring that would have meaning for such downcast people. What could he say that would have an impact on their lives?

But that evening as Moody brought the message, the entire atmosphere seemed charged with electricity, and

7

the congregation listened attentively and in quietness. In closing, he urged any who wanted "to have your lives changed by the power of God through faith in Jesus Christ as a personal Savior," wanted "to become Christians," to stand, so he could pray for them. People stood all over the chapel.

Astonished, Moody thought they had not understood and asked them to sit down. He stated again what becoming a Christian meant and then invited those who wished to do so to depart to an adjoining hall. He watched in amazement as scores of men, women, and older children made their way quietly to the connecting door. A schoolroom had been prepared for use as an inquiry room by setting out one or two dozen chairs. More chairs had to be added to seat the overflow crowd of people.

Addressing the crowd, Moody enlarged on repentance and faith, and again asked the people about becoming Christians. Once more, the whole room stood. In shock, Moody told them to meet with their minister the following night.

That Monday morning, he left London for another part of England, but on Tuesday, he received a telegram urging him to come back to the London church. More people had come to the minister's meeting on Monday night than had been in the room on Sunday!

Returning to London, Moody spoke at the Arundel Square Church each night for two weeks. Some fifty-three years later, a Baptist minister, James Sprunt, recalled that the results were staggering: "Four hundred were taken into the membership of that church, and by the grace of God I was one of that number."

Who was this rough, blustery, uneducated American? What brought him to London at such a time? What credentials did he possess that qualified him to preach to the dignified, reserved English? What message could he bring that they had not already heard?

Dwight Lyman Ryther Moody, born February 5, 1837, grew up in the gentle hill country of Northfield, Massachusetts. From birth, Dwight possessed a rugged constitution and determination to match. His happy-go-lucky father, Edwin, celebrated his son's birth with friends at the local pub.

A stonemason by trade, Edwin enjoyed drinking as well as the social life at the pub. He invited everyone to celebrate Dwight's birth with him: "C'mon, everyone. Have a glass of ale on me!" he bellowed. Of course, the pub patrons were only too happy to oblige. The people of Northfield liked Edwin: he was pleasant, hard-working, and easy to get along with. Because he disliked offending people, however, he often shrank from collecting debts owed him. This trait made paying his own bills more difficult. One more mouth to feed scarcely bothered Edwin. He enjoyed life and his family too much to give it a second thought.

The *Ryther* part of Dwight's name was dropped when the village doctor, Gideon Ryther, for whom he was named, failed to give the Moodys the expected sheep— the acceptable offering for being someone's namesake. The little boy became known simply as Dwight Lyman Moody.

The small town of Northfield, Massachusetts, was

located on both sides of the Connecticut River near the New Hampshire and Vermont borders and had a population of nearly seventeen hundred. During its early years, Northfield was known as *Squakeag,* an Indian name meaning *salmon.* The settlement's strategic location provided a primitive outpost to ward off French and Indian attacks.

The Moodys and Holtons, Dwight's ancestors, appear in Northfield's records nearly from the beginning. The Holtons settled in Northfield by 1672. Isaiah Moody, Dwight's grandfather, moved to Northfield in 1796 in order to practice his brick masonry trade; and Edwin, his first son, was born in 1800.

The two families were united when Dwight's parents were married on January 3, 1828; Betsey Holton was twenty-three, Edwin Moody, twenty-eight. The wedding had been scheduled for New Year's Day, but the Connecticut River unexpectedly thawed and overflowed its banks, so Edwin could not get to the wedding that day. But Edwin, despite this turn of events, detoured many miles, and two days later, married Betsey.

The young couple moved into an unpainted colonial house built by Edwin's cousin, Simeon Moody. Built at the north edge of town, the house lay at the base of a small, bald knoll in a treeless pasture and looked out over the Connecticut River.

The Moodys shared with their Northfield neighbors a quiet trust in God. After all, the Northfield Unitarian Church, even though cold and austere, was considered the center of the community, and membership was assumed for all proper citizens.

But Dwight's mother, Betsey, tall and stately, was really the strong spiritual force in the family's life. As her family began to grow she taught her children a little Bible lesson every day, and on Sundays she accompanied them to the Unitarian Sunday school. Betsey made all her boys swear vengeance on whiskey and everything that was an enemy to the family.

Like many other newlyweds of the time, the Moodys started married life fairly well off. Their relative prosperity continued during the early 1830s, but by 1836, the country found itself in a financial depression. Banks failed and a fourth of all businesses went bankrupt.

Northfield's local economy suffered, and Betsey and Edwin were forced to mortgage their home. They were unable to pay even the small annual $11.70 rent on pew thirteen in the Northfield Church. However, they did not despair. Betsey, an expert weaver, reassured Edwin, "We will manage somehow. The children can help out at some neighboring farms, and perhaps I can weave more items to sell."

"That's good," Edwin responded, "and my work looks promising. The Smiths told me they need a foundation for a new house they want to build. And there's some other projects coming along. Thank God, we have such good health—and our children, too."

That winter, finances still tight, Dwight was born. With four brothers and one sister, he had plenty of playmates. But he also learned from an early age to work hard on his parents' small farm. Sturdy and headstrong, dark-haired, brown-eyed Dwight always managed to be the person who took control of most situations. In fact, from the time he was little, Dwight had a bad temper when he didn't get his own way, and sometimes he got in trouble because of it. He even used a good bit of profanity in his early years, although his mother tried to cure him of it.

The Moody's financial situation continued to be precarious during the first four years of Dwight's life, and it seemed things couldn't get much worse. But when Dwight was just four years old, tragedy struck the family. Edwin had gone to work as usual and was laying brick when he was suddenly seized with an intense pain in his side. Staggering home, he groaned, "Oh, oh, my side hurts so much! Oh, Betsey, get the doctor, quick!" By one o'clock, Edwin's pain was much worse.

He stumbled toward his bed, fell on his knees, and died. Betsey, unaware of the seriousness of his illness, discovered his body and, as the realization of her terrible situation broke in upon her, she also became ill.

Everything changed for the Moody family following Edwin's death, and little Dwight sobbed as he thought, "What a pretty, sunshiny day for my father to fall suddenly dead!"

two

Childhood Years

F rom the time of Edwin Moody's death, the
Moody family struggled to cope with the loss of
their breadwinner. Astonished to see his mother's hair turn white almost overnight, Dwight knew the
family barely had enough food to eat. Not only that, but
they had little wood to burn in the fireplace, and it was
nearly as chilly inside as out. He didn't understand that
because of the heavy mortgage on the property, creditors
tried to take just about everything in the household.

One of the creditors, Richard Colton, came to the Moody
home as soon as he could following the funeral and took
most of the furniture, the horse and buggy, and the cows
(except for one calf he did not discover). The older boys
had hidden their father's tools, and only the dower
(widow's) law of Massachusetts prevented Mr. Colton
from turning the family out of the house.

A month after his father's death, Dwight's mother gave
birth to twins, a girl, Lizzie, and a boy, Samuel. Still in
bed following their birth, Betsey Moody was surprised to
see another creditor, rich Ezra Purple, come into her bedroom to collect the mortgage due on the house. Worse, he
wanted her to sign the house over to him! Betsey told Mr.
Purple that she would get the money as soon as she

could, but he didn't want to wait. Fortunately, two of Betsey's brothers, Charles and Cyrus Holton, were able to raise the needed mortgage funds for the rest of that year.

Dwight's four older brothers, Isaiah, George, Edwin, and Luther, soon found employment on nearby farms and helped support the family. But then fifteen-year-old Isaiah ran away from home. No one knew where Isaiah went or why. Probably the responsibilities that dropped on his shoulders following his father's premature death were simply too much for him.

Betsey continued to hope that her oldest son would come home. At night, she set a lantern in the west window to lure Isaiah back. Eagerly, she looked for news about him. She would send the children to the post office daily to see if he had written a letter. Dwight, his brothers, and his older sister, Cornelia, would come back and have to say, "No letter, today, Mother." When the family gathered in the evenings around the stone fireplace for Bible reading, Dwight's mother would lift her voice in prayer for Isaiah, calling him, "that wanderer." On Thanksgiving Day, she would always set a place for Isaiah, hoping it would be the day he returned.

Because of Mrs. Moody's difficult circumstances, many of the townspeople thought she should send all of her children except the twins to live elsewhere. But Dwight's mother wouldn't hear of it. She had already lost one son and was determined that with God's help and hard work, the family would manage. And manage they did, although as the boys got older, some of them began working at farms that were far enough away so they had to board with the farmer and only came home occasionally.

Little Dwight loved his family, and despite their hardships, he enjoyed the many good times they had together. Even though his mother spent considerable energy and time milking cows, weaving cloth, spinning yarn, and making the children's clothes, she still found time to be with each of her children.

Dwight knew, too, that if he disobeyed his mother—or the schoolmaster or any of his elders—his mother would have him pick out a strong, green switch from the backyard birch. That was one thing he could always count on—getting a good whipping for playing pranks on people or for being disobedient. But sometimes, it was hard for him to be good!

Dwight rarely suffered any guilt from his impish ways. Even though he and his family went to church regularly, it never occurred to him to call on God in his daily life. But once when he was six and herding cows to pasture, he got pinned under a fence rail. As he struggled unsuccessfully to lift the heavy rails, he began to panic and cry out: "Help me, somebody! Help!"

Nobody came. He began to think he might die. Then Dwight thought about God helping him and said, "God, help me lift these heavy rails." Right after his prayer, he found he could easily lift the rails.

When Dwight turned ten, his opportunity came to board and help with farmwork in Greenfield, Massachusetts. An older brother already worked in Greenfield doing chores for a farmer. This brother, who was constantly homesick, wrote frequent letters wanting Dwight to join him. And one cold day in November, he came home and announced that he had found a good place for Dwight—in Greenfield.

"Oh, how upset I was!" Dwight later wrote. "I didn't want to leave the comfort of my home, my mother, my brothers and sisters. I said I wouldn't go. But as mother and I sat by the fire, she said, 'Dwight, I think you will have to go. I don't think I shall be able to keep the family together this winter.'

"Mother's wish was enough. I didn't sleep much that night. I cried a great deal. The next morning after breakfast, I took my little bundle and started. About a mile from the house, my brother and I both sat down and cried. I thought I would never get back as long as I lived. We walked over the frozen ground about thirteen miles."

After the boys arrived in Greenfield and Dwight had been introduced to the old farmer he was to work for, he felt even stranger. "I was to milk the cows, go on errands, and go to school. But there were no children anywhere around! That afternoon, as I looked the old man over, I realized he didn't care for boys. Even though he was kinder than I first thought, he could not sympathize with a child. Later when I met his wife and looked her over, I thought she was more cross than he was. Oh, how homesick I was!"

But as Dwight did his chores well and pleased the farmer, his homesickness began to vanish. Then someone from a nearby town gave him a brand new penny, which was worth much more than today. To a young boy who rarely had any money, the penny represented a fortune. He thought he was rich!

"One thing that I learned from the old man and his penny was when you give anything to anybody, always do so in the name of Christ. Better still, tell the story of the cross and a loving heavenly Father. From that time on, I felt I at least had a friend in that little town."

After a while, Dwight was able to come back home. How happy he was to be back with those he loved, especially his mother. Although the family waged a constant struggle against poverty and sometimes lived for weeks on a diet of corn meal and milk, they were thankful. Dwight knew, too, that his mother would always find food for any poor person who stopped at their door. She taught each of her children to be generous with what they had.

Dwight's thankfulness extended to two other people who befriended his family. One was the minister, the Reverend Edward Everett, who watched out for the family, supplying what was needed, whether food, encouragement, prayer, or perhaps money. The church people, by and large, seemed indifferent to the Moody family's plight, so Dwight and his family were especially grateful to Pastor Everett for his concern.

Dwight's uncle, Cyrus Holton, proved to be a great help to the Moody family, as well. Dwight knew that when the wood bin was low, his mother would tell the children to stay in bed to keep warm until schooltime. But then, "I would hear the sound of chips flying, and I knew some one was chopping wood in our woodshed, and that we would soon have a fire. I shall never forget Uncle Cyrus coming with what seemed the biggest pile of wood I ever saw in my life."

Despite numerous hardships, Dwight managed to enjoy

many things. Shoes and stockings were luxuries reserved for Sundays, and Dwight carried them to within sight of the church before slipping them on. He reveled in sliding barefoot on the winter ice or racing along the dusty summer road. He was too busy having fun to mind the poverty that much.

With the first snowfall, the children brought their sleds out and delighted in sliding down the many hills surrounding Northfield. One day, Dwight and his friends saw an old gentleman who looked like Santa Claus driving an old dilapidated sleigh full of boys. They were hanging on to the runners and tying on ropes until there was a long string of sleds. This hilarious sight brought tears of laughter to Dwight and his friends.

Dwight possessed a competitive and sometimes mischievous spirit. He loved practical jokes. One time, a farmer for whom he worked was seated in his wagon. He asked Dwight for a jug of cider. Dwight happily obliged, but when the farmer put the jug to his lips, Dwight threw an apple at the horses. They bolted, the farmer flipped up in the air, the jug fell, and Dwight had to look for another job.

In addition to his fun-loving, mischievous nature, Dwight liked to bargain. One day when he was home by himself, he saw a band of gypsies approaching. Here was a golden opportunity. But what could he swap? His eyes lighted on the old swayback farm horse and then on the horse they had with them. He simply could not lose. Sure enough, the gypsies were agreeable, and soon Dwight was leading home a new horse, lank, rawboned, chopped-off tail, and all.

Thrilled with his bargain, he decided to put his prize to the test. Proudly he hitched the horse to the wagon with an empty barrel for a seat. He would go to town for the weekly supply of meal. The horse obediently rose to the occasion with a start and briskly galloped down the hill, but the sudden start caused Dwight and his barrel to be tossed out by the roadside.

Mrs. Moody sent her children to school, but Dwight's time in the classroom was limited because of his need to earn money in the fields and his impatience with book learning. In the schoolroom, the children sat in twos at their little desks, and while some baked by the nearby wood stove, others were chilled by the frigid drafts that shook the window panes and doorframe before blowing across the room.

When Dwight did attend school, his prankishness cut into his learning even more, and he received more than his share of whippings from the schoolmaster's "rattan" or rod. As Dwight said of him: "We had a man teacher who used the rattan on us a good deal and took us by the ears and twirled us around when we tried to do as we pleased." The boys pondered the ideal punishment for them. One faction said that love would do for them what the rattan failed to do while the other faction thought that the rattan was the only proper punishment. Generally, the rattan won out, especially over the good-sized school-boys.

The basic skills that Dwight absorbed from school were minimal. His penmanship, nearly indecipherable, became legible by its size rather than by its neatness. From *McGuffey's Rhetorical Guide Number Five,* he learned the principles of elocution, which proved useful later in his life. However, two areas he failed to master were spelling and grammar. A sample letter he wrote at seventeen illustrates his lack in these skills:

> *I was happy to here from home every weak, but you ned not think that I am homesick. . .the time goes by lik a whirl wind how do the things look have you any pears yet Where I bord there is over 50 now and lots of them about my age.*

Once, incredibly, Dwight even won a spelling bee! But having little time to study to master basic skills, he became increasingly impatient with school. By the sixth grade, he decided he had had enough of it and left school for good.

Of course, churchgoing tried energetic Dwight perhaps more than school did. His mother insisted that all her children be regular in church attendance. But Dwight showed his reluctance: "I used to look upon Sunday with a certain amount of dread. I don't know that the minister even noticed me, unless it was when I was asleep in the gallery and he woke me up." Then he adds, "It was hard to have to work in the field all the week, and then be obliged to go to church and hear a sermon I didn't understand."

Between his frustration with church, school, and having to work so hard, the time was ripe for Dwight to do something different and see new sights. Since the railroad had come to Northfield when he was eleven, he began to wonder about the world that lay beyond his hometown—at the end of the railroad tracks. It was just a matter of time before the desire to find out got the best of him, and he made up his mind to leave Northfield for good.

three

City Life

On a blustery February day in 1854, seventeen-year-old Dwight Lyman Moody sat in a train car en route to the big city of Boston. His jaw was set firmly, his homespun clothes patched and fairly wrinkle-free as he gazed out the window at the passing landscape.

"I will make a new life for myself in Boston—where I don't have to do all those dirty, old farm chores like putting up hay and milking cows all the time. I'll buy some new clothes, see some new things, and. . .and I'll meet some new people. And I'll be successful!" he murmured to himself as the train clacked and jerked along on the sometimes bumpy rails.

Dwight reveled in the journey as the speeding train carried him farther and farther from the small village of Northfield. But a gnawing sensation in the pit of his stomach reminded him that he faced an unfamiliar and uncertain life ahead. Suddenly, the train would lurch, the whistle shriek, and the bell clang as it passed one sleepy hamlet after another.

He remembered his mother's words uttered with choked emotion: "Please, Dwight, don't leave Northfield just yet. Maybe you can find some work besides those farm chores you hate so much. We don't want you to go far away! Besides, I need you to stay close by and help with the rest of the family." She had sobbed, clinging tightly to him.

But he had made up his mind. Whatever misgivings he had about leaving Northfield and going to Boston he kept to himself. The previous Thanksgiving, he had even asked his uncle Samuel Socrates Holton about a position in his shoe store: "Uncle," he faltered at the dining table, "I want to come to Boston, and have a place in your shoe-store. Will you take me?"

Every eye at the table had fastened on young Dwight. Squirming uncomfortably, he'd looked from face to face.

Uncle Samuel cleared his throat and looked across the table at Dwight's mother. "Shall I take him?"

Twenty-one-year-old brother George blurted out, "No! he'll soon want to run your store!" As Dwight's brown eyes continued to scrutinize each face and glimpsed amusement, consternation, or contempt on each one, they rested finally on Aunt Typhenia, Uncle Samuel's young, second wife. Her eyes offered sympathy and understanding, traits the young Dwight would always hold dear. But nothing was settled for him at that time. He would have to wait until he finally got to Boston.

His thoughts returning to the present, Dwight nervously fingered the five-dollar bill his brother Ed had pressed into his hand. Ed wasn't so hard-hearted after all, he mused. He had regretted all the tearful good-byes though. But they couldn't be helped. He was going to Boston to make his fortune, and that was that.

Shortly after the Central Vermont train chugged into

the station, a confident Dwight marched down to Court Street and Uncle Samuel's shoe store. Uncle Samuel, both surprised and alarmed to see him, found himself at a complete loss of words when confronted with young Dwight's request for employment. After inquiring about the family's health and other matters, he gave no other response. But Uncle Lemuel, his partner in the shoe business, suggested that Dwight stay with him in suburban Winchester while looking for work.

Dwight left the store with a smug look on his face and a swagger in his step. He knew that Uncle Samuel would soon feel chagrin at having missed out on such a good assistant!

But as Dwight stopped at store after store and shop after shop, he realized that there were more people available for jobs than there were jobs to be had.

Many Irish immigrants had come to Boston following the potato famine in Ireland. All of these people were looking for work. Dwight's confidence in finding a job began to lag. By the afternoon of the second day he was miserable and said later, "The feeling. . .that no one wanted you. I shall never forget those two dark days. Oh, the sadness, the loneliness."

He drifted to the docks and pondered signing on as a sailor. He also haunted the post office, hoping for a letter from Northfield. His little twelve-year-old sister Lizzie wrote him warning him about pickpockets, but Dwight's pockets were as empty as his stomach.

Trudging back to his Uncle Lemuel, he made a vow, promising God that "if He would give me work, I would love and serve Him." But when he saw Uncle Lemuel, he was defiant. "I'm going to walk to New York!" he exclaimed.

Wise Uncle Lemuel realized that Dwight's pride had nearly broken and advised him to "ask your Uncle Samuel for a job, but be direct about it."

Dwight hesitated. "He knows perfectly well what I want."

Again, Uncle Lemuel urged, "Go on, ask him!"

His uncle won out, and a humbled Dwight sought out Uncle Samuel. Uncle Samuel responded with a long, thoughtful stare.

At last he said, "Dwight, I'm afraid that if you come to work here you will soon want to run the store yourself. Now my men do the work as I want it done." Then he decreed some regulations, laid down certain conditions, and suggested that Dwight think them over during the weekend.

Dwight blurted out, "I don't want to wait till Monday. I promise now!"

The following week Dwight wrote a letter to his family:

> *I do not bord out to Uncle SS [Samuel]
> now I bord in the city Calvin and I are
> going to room together bimb bi that word
> is not spelt rite I guess. I have a room up
> in the third story and I can open my
> winder and there is 3 grat buildings full of
> girls the handsomest thare is in the city
> they will swar like parrets.*

Like his mother, Dwight eliminated most punctuation

marks in his writing and also spelled words as they sounded to him, in a dialect and idiom of the Connecticut Valley.

Dwight soon entered into Boston's community life. His gregarious, although blunt, sometimes downright tactless ways, soon gained him many friends—along with a few enemies.

In summer, he delighted in running free across Boston Common—a pastime enjoyed by numerous other newcomers. And in winter, tobogganing captured some of his scant leisure time, but he also watched rich boys race on their highly polished sleds.

Not only did Dwight join in more acceptable kinds of sports, but he relished a good fistfight as well. He remarked later about his many scraps: "I used to have a terrible habit of swearing. Whenever I would get mad, out would come the oaths"—and up would come his fists, ready to slug it out with any and all comers.

Most of all, playing practical jokes ranked number one with Dwight: "I was full of animal life, and shut up in the store through the day and sleeping there at night I had to have some outlet, and used to lie awake at nights to think of some new joke to play upon somebody."

One of the somebodies turned out to be the Italian cobbler who worked in the shoe store: "Although the cobbler liked me he had such an awful temper that my joking came near costing my life. One day I fitted a lady with an expensive pair of shoes and he was changing the buttons when enraged by some trick I played upon him, he seized the knife and sprang at me and for a few minutes I had all I could do to keep out of his reach."

Life as a salesman greatly pleased Dwight. Instead

of performing unsavory farm chores, he charmed and persuaded people to buy more and costlier shoes. He competed subtly with the other clerks to be the top salesman and reveled in the continuous challenges.

For the first time in his life, he had money, although not all that much. He sent a portion home to his mother informing her that, "I would not go back again to live for nothing." Then he added triumphantly, "I never enjoyed myself so well be for in my life the time goes like a whirl wind."

Despite new opportunities, Dwight missed his family and at times experienced considerable loneliness.

Scolding his brother George, he wrote, "I wish the duse you would some of you write to me." Another time, he admonished, "What in thunder the reason was I did not get a letter this morning I could not make out. . .I should like to go home this year if I could git away but it is all in vain can't wright any more so goodby resp. yours Dwight L. Moody."

When Uncle Samuel laid down his rules and regulations for Dwight, he included his attendance at Mount Vernon Street Orthodox Church. Coming from his more liberal Unitarian background, Dwight was now confronted, probably for the first time, with the claims of Jesus Christ as his personal Savior.

Uncle Samuel had also insisted that Dwight enroll in Sunday school, and he was assigned to Edward Kimball's class. Attending the first time, Dwight was handed a Bible and told to find the Gospel of John. As he thumbed anxiously through Genesis, the other boys began to snicker at his ignorance. Wisely, Kimball reproved the boys with a glance and quietly exchanged Bibles with Dwight, giving him one marked at the correct place. Dwight's gratefulness became apparent when he told a close friend later that he would "stick by the fellow who had stood by him and had done him a turn like that."

Uncle Samuel suggested to the deacons that Dwight's lack of Bible knowledge was his mother's fault. But that wasn't true. He simply daydreamed through most Bible readings at home, and since grimy youngsters' hands were forbidden to touch the Bible, he failed to glean much Bible knowledge.

Over the next eleven months, Dwight listened to sermon after sermon from Dr. Edward Norris Kirk. The church itself had been formed twelve years earlier by Bostonians unhappy with the rigid doctrinal exclusiveness of another large city church. Pastor Kirk emphasized the sinfulness of man and man's inability to save himself. He spoke of Christ's death on the cross for all mankind, of Christ's resurrection from the dead, and of Christ's desire to be the friend of each one who trusted Him. On the other hand, the minister issued dire warnings to all who refused so great a salvation, and he verbally assaulted those who failed to do so.

Over the next eleven months as Pastor Kirk's messages and Edward Kimball's teaching combined in Dwight's mind, he found himself caught up in a spiritual struggle: "I thought I would wait till I died and then become a Christian. I thought if I had the consumption or some lingering disease, I would have plenty of time to become one, and in the meantime I would enjoy the best of the pleasures of the world."

Repeatedly stressing that the spiritual issue was one of choice and of yielding one's will to Another, Kirk emphasized that this choice led to a life of faith. Young Dwight sensed the minister was right, yet he seemed unable to yield his will to God.

Then in April, Mount Vernon Church held a revival. And on Saturday, April 21, 1855, Edward Kimball resolutely decided to speak to his recalcitrant Sunday school pupil about his soul.

Arriving at the store, he found that Dwight was in the back, wrapping shoes. He didn't want to embarrass him, however, and almost had decided to come back at a more convenient time. "I began to wonder whether I ought to go just then during business hours," he later reported. "And I thought maybe my mission might embarrass the boy, that when I went away the other clerks might ask who I was, and when they learned might taunt Moody and ask if I was trying to make a good boy out of him. Then, I decided to make a dash for it and have it over at once."

Going over to Dwight in the back of the shoe store, "I placed my hand on his shoulder, leaned over, and placed my foot on a shoe box."

Kimball looked into Dwight's eyes and "asked him to come to Christ, who loved him and who wanted his love and should have it."

Dwight's struggle came to a head, and he surrendered his will to God's will and came to Christ through Kimball's invitation.

"My plea was a very weak one," Kimball observed later, "but I was sincere." He also realized, "The young man was just ready for the light that broke upon him. For there, at once, in the back of that shoe store in Boston, Dwight gave himself and his life to Christ."

The following morning as he left his room, Dwight's happiness and peace knew no bounds. The wide grin on his face and the fresh sparkle in his big brown eyes reflected his newfound joy. He sensed, "The old sun shone a good deal brighter than it ever had before—I felt that it was just smiling upon me; and as I walked out upon Boston Common and heard the birds singing in the trees, I thought they were all singing a song to me."

As he marched along, it seemed all creation cheered him on his way, and he sensed that "I had not a bitter feeling against any man, and I was ready to take all men to heart."

Then Dwight's thoughts turned to his family, his mother, brothers, and sisters, and he began "then and there to pray for them," realizing with sadness that he had never prayed for them before.

He had tried to help his family in different ways, sending not only money but also shoes which he purchased at trade prices. Along with his gifts, Dwight generally offered his sage opinions about everything. Now, he thought, "I could tell them what God has done for me. I thought I would only have to explain it to have them all see the light."

Visiting home a short time later to help put in the potato and watermelon crops, Dwight attempted to tell his family about his newfound faith. They looked at him blankly, and his mother declared fervently, "I will remain a Unitarian the rest of my life!" They thought Dwight had gotten into some strange doctrine in Boston.

Heavyhearted, Dwight returned to Boston and soon appeared before the Mount Vernon Church board for membership. Not until the applicant answered the board's questions satisfactorily would he be admitted to membership.

Sitting in front of the austere board, Dwight suffered from extreme nervousness: his dry mouth felt as though it was stuffed with cotton. His palms were sweating, and his knees would have knocked together had he been standing. His normal joviality had deserted him in the presence of this august company.

"Ah, Mr. Moody," began Deacon Higginbottom, "Have you been awakened? Did you see yourself as a sinner? Do you feel dependent on Christ for forgiveness?"

Dwight found himself at a complete loss for words. His inadequate guttural responses consisted of "Yes," "No," and "Sure," which the clerk quickly remedied into correct doctrinal statements.

In exasperation, the chairman rose from his seat and, glowering down on poor Dwight, fairly shouted, "Mr. Moody, what has Christ done for us all—for you— which entitles Him to our love?"

Hesitatingly, his head hung low, Dwight stammered, "I. . .I don't know. I think Christ has done a good deal for us. But I don't think of anything particular as I know of."

Admission was denied, and the church assigned two pious deacons to teach Dwight the principles of the faith. Dwight would have none of it, avoiding the two well-intentioned men like the plague. As he remarked to a friend, "You might as well try to get a man to go before a Justice of the Peace."

The next March, the church finally granted Dwight admission, although as Kimball conceded, "Little more light had appeared."

Many years later, the officials at Mount Vernon Church were the ones to hang their heads in shame over their misjudgment of Dwight Moody. By then, they would have gladly sat at his feet.

But as Kimball pointed out at the time, the main proofs that Dwight had become a Christian were slim: he no longer swore, and he said the Bible had changed from being dull and dry to being his favorite book.

Nineteen years old and managing another shoe store for his uncle, Dwight suddenly found Boston stifling. The set ways, the tradition, the old established business houses, the rigid manners and proper social mores discouraged him at every turn. Everything he had thrilled over when he first came to Boston lay in ashes at his feet.

He was ready for a change, and after he and Uncle Samuel had a falling out over Dwight's request for a raise, he struck out in September 1856 for the booming prairie city of Chicago.

four

D wight left Boston with mixed emotions. Once more, he had little money but high hopes. His mother didn't know of his new plans to leave Boston, so he wrote her a letter telling her of his decision: "Uncle S.S. objected to my going, but I was fairly drove out of Boston." Evidently Uncle Samuel had not approved of his nephew's plans to go farther west but also refused to increase his salary.

Dwight paid five dollars for his ticket on an immigrant train which took him within twenty miles of his Northfield home. Sadly, he couldn't even stop to say good-bye to his family.

Arriving in Chicago, Dwight's spirits lifted. Another uncle, jovial Uncle Calvin Holton, soon arranged a position for him with Wiswall's shoe store on Lake Street.

He quickly got involved in various activities. The first week after his arrival, he met a Mr. King, a lawyer, at prayer meeting. Mr. King's impression of Dwight provides an interesting observation: "Mr. Moody is one of the happiest looking people I ever saw. His cheeks are full, so red and rosy, and he possesses such a pleasant smile and look, he attracted much attention."

Chicago and Dwight formed an almost immediate bond. He relished nearly every aspect of this sprawling, raucous city. Its stockyards, slaughterhouses, and tanneries filled the air with foul odors; factories and foundries saturated the atmosphere with pungent, thick smoke; and Lake Michigan coated Chicago with mud. But none of Chicago's citizens cared. Like Dwight, they appeared to thrive on all their city's seemingly offensive elements.

Writing home, Dwight exclaimed: "The streets are all lade out strate and broad. You can stand and look as far as the eye can reach and try to walk out of the city." Neither were the buildings as close together as Boston's. Even so, fires were frequent and devastating. Hungry flames would leap from building to building, devouring entire city blocks befoe being brought under control.

It wasn't long before Dwight found himself caught up in one of Chicagoans' main goals: making money. Tops in selling shoes, he also benefitted from personal habits of thrift and exactness. Soon these traits combined with an intense ambition to possess large sums of money.

Because of Dwight's energy and enthusiasm, Wiswell's shoe store appointed him to meet immigrant trains and sell boots to the newcomers. His plain speech and friendly grin worked like a charm to make sales. So intent was he on making money, Dwight prayed that "God would give me one hundred thousand dollars."

He wrote to his mother cheerfully: "I can make money faster here thin I can in B. I have one of the best situations in the city. I hav done the very best thing in coming here." Some of Dwight's money-making strategies included putting his savings into land, then selling it at a profit. He also made loans at high rates. He was well on his way to becoming a millionaire.

His brother George received a letter from him exulting in Chicago's opportunities: "I tell you, hear is the place to make money, and that is not all. I have enjoyed more Religion hear thean I have ever in my life. I find the better I live the more enjoyment I have."

The city of Chicago also experienced a spiritual revival early in 1857. Dwight's natural enthusiasm now turned to taking part in the revival. Renting four pews at Plymouth Church, he filled them with young men from Wiswall's shoe store and other nearby stores, and sometimes with people simply walking by the church. On Sunday afternoons, Dwight and a friend often passed out religious literature to sailors and in saloons, boarding houses, and the shacks of many poor people.

Dwight wanted so much to share his faith! But his efforts in church always seemed to be thwarted. "I want so much to be part of Plymouth Church," he confided to a new friend. His downfall always came when he opened his mouth and his poor speech came tumbling out. He noticed how people "squirmed their shoulders when I get up to pray at prayer meeting." The church board even notified Uncle Calvin, forbidding Dwight to speak at church because his grammar was too poor!

A new position opened for Dwight near the end of 1857. He became a traveling salesman and debt collector for the wholesale boot and shoe house of C. H. Henderson. His brother Luther, visiting him in Chicago, told him, "Dwight, I think it's foolish of you to leave such a secure position with Wiswall. Are you sure you're doing the right thing?"

"I have got me a situation that is worth five of that and

35

if I have my health and my God is with me I shall suck-seed better here in Chicago than ever I thought I should," boasted Dwight confidently. With that, Dwight was off and running, soon covering the six states of Missouri, Iowa, Wisconsin, Indiana, Michigan, and Illinois.

He loved his new job, calling it "better than anything I have ever done—it is nothing but excitement all the time!" This job made him even more prosperous, and when back in Chicago, he boarded at an excellent boarding house run by Mrs. Hubert Phillips. Many of Chicago's fashionable young bachelors roomed there as well; Dwight's social status had greatly improved.

In his spare time, Dwight sought for a Christian activity in Chicago. Someone suggested he go to Wells Street Mission and ask the people there if he could help with something. When he told the man in charge that he couldn't teach, the man said offhandedly, "Why don't you go out into the alleys and streets to see what boys you can bring in?"

With that directive, Dwight set out to see what boys he could find. Rounding up eighteen ragged, barefoot boys on his first trip to Chicago's seamier side, Dwight joyfully delivered them to the Well's Street Mission. Dressed in a checkered gray suit which covered his stocky frame, Dwight no doubt impressed the boys. He asked them: "Don't you want to go with me to Sunday school?" One of the boys replied, "Are you going to have a picnic?"

Dwight responded, "Come along with me and we will find out." Later Dwight confessed, "That was the happiest Sunday I have ever known! After searching for two years trying to find out what my work was before I succeeded, I finally had found out what my mission was."

Like everything he did, Dwight threw himself wholeheartedly into this new venture of "finding boys."

"Notwithstanding his crude and somewhat uncouth appearance, we became close friends at once," one of the boys remembered about Moody in his later years. "And we found him to be a most agreeable companion—good humored, ready and witty in speech, simple, unaffected and kind, with a charm of manner and a personality so winning and interesting that we all immediately swore allegiance to our new found stranger friend."

Calling his new occupation "drumming up scholars," Dwight often appeared late for the Methodist Episcopal young men's class on Sunday mornings. He had joined the class much to the consternation of his fellow Congregationalists at Plymouth Church.

Another class member, John V. Farwell, disdained the young man who came late to class every Sunday. Farwell, one of the most successful and wealthy men in the city, had arrived in Chicago on a hay wagon with four dollars to his name. At thirty-three, he now owned the leading store in Chicago. But when another class member mentioned to Farwell that "young Moody brings all these ragamuffin boys to Wells Street Mission every Sunday before class," Farwell felt ashamed.

His criticism of Dwight turned back to himself as he wondered why "I wasn't doing something for others as well as this young man?" Soon after that, the two men became good friends, and Farwell began to help in Dwight's enterprises.

As Dwight came with his boys to the Wells Street Mission one Sunday, he glimpsed a new teacher for the girls, a good-looking young woman who possessed grace and elegance. He had noticed her a few years earlier at another church.

Although only fifteen, Emma Revell seemed mature beyond her years, and almost before he realized it, Dwight found himself calling at the Washington Street home of Fleming H. Revell, a recent English emigrant. Emma's open acceptance of Dwight in spite of his uncouth, awkward ways won his heart early on.

In spite of his romantic interest, Dwight soon faced a new dilemma.

five

Widening Horizons

Many of the boys Dwight brought to the Wells Street Mission lived in the Sands, an area near Lake Michigan. The tumbledown shacks were crowded with German and Irish immigrants, many of whom suffered from the ravages of joblessness and whiskey. Their poverty was extreme.

Some of the first boys Dwight brought to the mission had dropped out a short time later due to lack of interest. Dwight's traveling schedule always affected the boys' attendance, and after he was gone a few weeks, they simply stopped coming.

As Dwight rode the train on his various travels, he thought repeatedly about the boys like Jimmy Sexton and Tom Stevens who existed in ignorance and poverty. *Why doesn't the church reach out to the adults in these areas?* he wondered. Of course, Dwight also realized that the boys didn't care for the formality and rote learning of the Wells Street Mission. He could hardly blame them—he never cared much for it either.

Back in Chicago in 1858, Dwight had an idea! He and an architect friend obtained an abandoned freight car on North State Street. After rounding up several boys, Dwight asked them, "How'd you boys like to help us start a mission Sunday school?"

Jimmy Sexton piped up excitedly: "That would be great! We'd be like co-partners, wouldn't we? And we'd have a chance to be the boss sometimes, too, wouldn't we?"

The following Sunday, the new mission got under way amid shouts and cheers from numerous boys. A young businessman with a fine voice was brought in to lead the music, but the boys needed to be taught most of the hymns.

Before long, as the boys brought other friends to the new mission, the car became so jam-packed, it nearly burst at the seams. When some of Dwight's friends learned of the crowded conditions, they wanted to help, so they obtained a one-and-a-half-story house on Michigan Street for the mission. The house was a former saloon that was now in disuse; Dwight used the large front room and a store at the back.

The numbers of boys continued to increase. Sometimes when Dwight was in town during the week, he would have extra meetings which he conducted himself. On one occasion, a Thanksgiving Day service, Dwight had invited his friend G. S. F. Savage to join him. When Mr. Savage arrived, he found the place dark. He recalled later: "There were no gas fixtures in the house, and he was trying to light it with a half-dozen candles, but the darkness had rather the best of it. I found him with a candle in one hand and a Bible in the other, and a child on his knee who he was trying to teach."

Mr. Savage added: "There were twenty-five or thirty children in all, and they were as sorry a lot of little ragamuffins as could have been found in Chicago." But to

Dwight, these children were precious jewels, and they made up the mission to which God had called him.

Increasingly, Dwight found himself hindered from the work he loved by his traveling job. He would be gone for nearly a month and missed three out of every four Sundays in Chicago, but he felt loyal to his employer, Mr. Henderson, for he treated Dwight as he would his own son.

Another reason Dwight wished to remain in Chicago was Emma. He visited the Revell house frequently, and Emma's little nine-year-old brother, Fleming, would hide behind the stove and listen to their conversation. He was usually disappointed because Dwight generally brought at least two other young men with him since Emma had two sisters, Anna and Sarah.

If it is true that opposites attract, the love between Emma and Dwight can be easily explained. Emma earned her living as a teacher, and though her father never made much money, their Washington Street home displayed culture and hospitality and reflected their English roots.

While Dwight seemed charged with health and vigor, Emma suffered from asthma and headaches. Shy and retiring, Emma enjoyed being around the extroverted Dwight. He was impulsive, outspoken, dominant, and had little education. Emma was intensely conventional, conservative, far better educated, fond of reading, possessed discriminating taste, and was self-effacing. Yet they seemed made for each other, and Dwight fell head over heels in love with her.

Dwight's life took another turn when his employer died suddenly in late 1858. Because of a difference of opinion with the new management, Dwight left the firm, going with Buell, Hill, and Granger. Several months later, Mrs. Henderson pleaded with Dwight to help them get rid of the incompetent administration of Henderson's estate, to collect the debts, and to wind up the estate. Although he felt honored, Dwight felt, "I was not old enough to take such an estate on my shoulders but they insisted I was." He didn't comply with Mrs. Henderson's wishes, however. Part of the reason lay in his increasing disregard for business.

Once more, the Sunday school mission outgrew its facilities, and Dwight's friends helped him obtain larger quarters. The lawyer Mr. King told another friend, "I became so greatly impressed with the great work, and Moody's earnestness and devotion to it convinced me that I in my humble way should do something similar." So King took Moody to the former mayor of Chicago, "Long" John Wentworth. Through Wentworth's influence, Dwight secured another building for the mission, a hall built on the site of the old North Market.

The meeting room upstairs had a huge grimy hall with blackened walls and ceiling. It was bare and uninviting. The area underneath was occupied with the local fire truck, and periodically, the school session would be interrupted by firemen harnessing their horses, a puffing engine boiler being stoked to get up steam and pump the hose, and the noise of clanging bells as the horses galloped away with the fire engine.

On Saturday nights the German society held dances in the North Market Hall. They would pile up the school chairs and other materials in a heap, and they left the floor a mess of cigar stubs, ashes, beer puddles, and papers. Since Dwight refused to employ labor on Sunday, he would do the cleaning himself no matter how late he returned from traveling Saturday night. Jimmy Sexton had been assigned to help Dwight. He felt the work was "as dirty, disagreeable, and unpleasant a chore as could be imagined. But I considered myself well paid with an approving word of encouragement from Mr. Moody."

Following the cleanup, Dwight would rush outside to drum up the pupils along with new boys and the girls who were also coming. If he needed to, Dwight would reason with children's parents to permit them to come, and he would even wash and dress the youngsters if necessary.

Given the large numbers, it was imperative that the children be divided into classes. Again, Dwight pressed his friends into teaching the classes, telling them they would be teaching "lambs."

The school grew to six hundred students. Dwight appointed a banker friend, Isaac Burch, as superintendent, and later gave the position to his friend John Farwell. But he, himself, was the one in charge. Each of the children thought of Dwight as their personal friend.

After being gone on a lengthy trip, he wrote one of his brothers, "I shall expect to have a good time next Sunday when I get home, for I have been away some time now and the children are so glad to see me when I return. I think I have got the best school there is in the west; anyway, it is the largest school there is this side of N. York." Only John Wanamaker had a bigger one; it was in Philadelphia.

"Full speed ahead" seemed to be the motto of Dwight's

life. The school—and his "scholars"—had brought a new impetus to his life. He had so much to do now that he knew what his mission was! But his heart filled with praise to God as he thought to himself: "How good You are Lord; I just praise You for all You have done for me!" Now, he wanted to return his gratitude to God by doing the one thing he knew to do. He had reached a few youngsters through the mission, but there were so many more to be reached!

Dwight confided to a friend the school made him think of those steamboats on the Mississippi that must either go fast or burst. His letters home reflected his constant movement and energy as he would scribble, "I am in a great hurry," or, "I am in such a hurry tonight you must excuse me for not writing more this time I am in a hurry!" Dwight sensed there was scarcely time enough to do all that needed to be done.

Dwight didn't consider himself able to speak or to teach. He believed his part was simply to round up as many youngsters as he could and let someone else do the speaking and teaching. But sometimes if no speaker came, he had to fill in. At first, the polish and length of contemporary sermons intimidated him; if a minister was present, Dwight became extremely nervous. Eventually he found himself able to talk to an audience of children.

Doing something he enjoyed doing, such as simply telling boys and girls Bible stories or talking about Bible characters as though they were someone living down the street, became easier and easier for Dwight. Before long, he desired to speak and to share. It was as though the love of God had welled up and began to overflow, and the dam inside him had burst.

Everywhere Dwight went, he would begin to teach and preach about God's love in Christ. Whether he was on a train and had a short layover where he could gather a small crowd, or in larger groups, he relished the opportunity to tell others what Christ had done in his life.

He had shared with many people by this time, but he yearned to go home and tell his family about Christ. In preparation, he wrote his brother George in November 1859, "You seame to think that there is some humbug about my coming home, but I think there is no dout but that I shall be to home next month with out fail if not in January shure." Arriving in Northfield two months later, Dwight had issued fair warning to its Unitarian inhabitants that "there is nothing like the religion of Jesus Christ."

Even Uncle Zebulon Allen expressed concern following Dwight's trip home: "My nephew Dwight is crazy, crazy as a March hare. Came on from Chicago last week for a flying visit. I had not seen him, but he drove into my yard this morning. You know how cold it was, and his face was as red as red flannel. Before I could say good morning, he shouted 'Good morning, Uncle Zebulon, What are you going to do for Christ today?' Of course, I was startled and finally managed to say, 'Come in, Dwight, and we will talk it over.' 'No, I can't stop, but I want you to think about it,' and he turned the sleigh around and went up the hill like a streak of lightning. I tell you he is crazy." Dwight left a mark on Northfield after that visit!

Not only Northfield felt the fire of this young evangelist. Everywhere Dwight went, he touched people for Christ.

On one occasion, he spoke to a banker on the train about his need for salvation: "Did you ever think what a good heavenly Father we have to give us such a pleasant world to live in?" Dwight asked the stranger. The response, "Yes, indeed."

Dwight: "Are you a Christian?"

The banker: "No."

Dwight: "You are not a Christian? But you ought to be one at once. I get off at the next station. If you will kneel down right here, I will pray to the Lord to make you a Christian."

So they knelt, and Dwight prayed, and the banker prayed. At the train stop, Dwight called back to the banker, "Remember, my friend, now is the time to accept."

In a daze, the banker shouted after him, "Tell me who you are!"

"My name is Moody."

In Chicago sometime later, the banker, Mr. Reynolds, found out where Dwight held his meetings. As he entered the building, "the first thing I saw was a man standing up, with a few tallow candles around him, holding a [black] boy, and trying to read to him the story of the Prodigal Son."

Mr. Reynolds became one of Dwight's staunch supporters, and he delighted in telling friends who were puzzled by his sudden conversion about the meeting on the train with Dwight Moody. He also invited Dwight to come to the country and speak to some people there.

Since Dwight now worked on a part-time commission basis and earned nearly as much as he had before, he had more time to accept opportunities such as that of Reynolds. He would have been content to continue to finance his Christian endeavors with his own money had not God intervened through one of his mission teachers.

On a beautiful June day in 1860, Dwight was working in his office at Buell, Hill, and Granger when the door suddenly swung open and a pale young man staggered in. Without saying a word, he threw himself down on some nearby boxes.

six

Children's Friend

A mazed, Dwight gasped, "What's wrong?"
His friend's response: "I have been bleeding at the lungs, and the doctor says that living on Lake Michigan is bad for me. I need to return to New York State—probably to die."

The teacher's ghastly white face and shaken demeanor startled Dwight even more. "What is the matter? Are you afraid to die?"

Again, the teacher shook his head. "Oh, no, sir. But I'm concerned for my class."

Dwight knew the class was made up of frivolous girls from twelve to sixteen. On one occasion, he had had to take the class, and their silly prattling and marching around the room nearly caused him to say, "Leave, and don't come back!"

Now the teacher's real concern came out: "I'm burdened for my class. I have failed them—not one of them has been led to Jesus. Now my strength is gone. I have done the girls more harm than good. How can I face God? Not one of the girls has been converted!"

Dwight listened attentively but with perplexity. He had never heard anyone talk in this manner. His entire effort had concentrated on the numbers of students in the mission. His heart thrilled each time he looked at overflowing crowds, at hundreds of noisy children, and he would be downcast when the numbers dropped even the slightest. He hadn't considered that his wild, young charges could experience conversion like adults; he hadn't thought of them as individuals.

Then Dwight suggested to the teacher, "Why don't you go around and tell them how you feel? If you want, I will go with you in a carriage."

After assisting the man to the street and hiring a carriage, Dwight accompanied his friend to the shabby part of Chicago. As they reached the tenement home of the first girl, the teacher rasped weakly, "I have come just to ask you to come to the Savior." The girl listened with rapt attention as he shared that he must leave Chicago and would die. He urged her to put her trust in Christ. Then, as the teacher prayed, the girl tearfully agreed to settle the question of salvation then and there.

Following this encounter, the men climbed back into the carriage and rode to another girl's home. The teacher again pressed the claims of Christ on this girl, telling her he would be leaving Chicago to die. After making a few calls, he was exhausted, so Dwight drove him home.

Ten days later, Dwight was at work when the teacher "came to the store with his face literally shining. He told me, 'The last one of my class has yielded herself to Christ. The great vital question of their lives is settled. They have accepted my Savior. My work is done, and I am going home.' "

But Dwight urged him to wait for a day. Then he suggested getting the entire class together and bringing them over for tea.

That evening, each of the girls and the teacher came to Dwight's place. Then the teacher read some Scripture and spoke to them, after which the girls sang a parting hymn. As they knelt to pray, the teacher pleaded with God to deepen the girls' newfound faith. Dwight prayed next and was just rising from his knees when one of the girls began to pray for her dying teacher.

Amazed, Dwight listened to the faltering, spontaneous prayer of a slum girl whom he had known to be an empty-headed scoffer. Another girl prayed asking God for power to win others to Himself. One after another, the girls halt-ingly prayed. As Dwight listened incredulously to these genuine, fervent thanksgivings, these earnest petitions, the hundred thousand gold dollars of his dreams turned to tinsel; his ambition to build a commercial empire appeared tawdry and fleeting. All at once, he found him-self weighing the desires of the world for wealth and power against the things of eternity. He would rather spend the rest of his years as this dying teacher had spent the past ten days.

The following evening, Dwight hurried to the railway station to see his friend off. Incredibly, without any pre-arranged plans, each of the girls came to the station to say good-bye to their teacher. They sang a hymn, and as the train rolled out of the depot, Dwight remarked later, "We could see the teacher's pale hand pointing towards the heaven where he wished to meet them."

The impact of this entire episode on Dwight was tremendous. It proved to be God's way of drawing on his heart strings to leave the business world, but he struggled for over three months before he arrived at a decision. He did not want to leave business! He relished the give and take and challenges of business, especially the competitiveness involved in salesmanship. As he thought afterward: "I fought against it. It was a terrible battle. But oh! how many times I have thanked God's will."

He faced losing the prestige of wealth in a city that only recognized wealth. Then, too, he would have to postpone marriage and be able to offer Emma only a small income when they did marry. His main struggle, however, was over leaving the business world. Emma would understand, but to lose face in the business world simply by bowing out. . .it was nearly unthinkable. At last, Dwight decided to leave Buell, Hill, and Granger. He realized he couldn't serve God and mammon; one had to have first place in his life.

Dwight hadn't shared his long, difficult struggle with anyone, but in the fall of 1860, his friend J. V. Farwell discovered that Dwight had left both his place of employment and Mrs. Phillips' exclusive boardinghouse. Dwight was sleeping on a settee in one of the rooms used by the YMCA in the Methodist Church block. Instead of nourishing his quite hefty frame in fine restaurants, he ate either in cheap diners or managed on cheese and crackers. Dwight determined to stretch his savings. He told himself, "I'll live on what I've saved. When that is gone and there is no means of support, I'll take it as a call to return to business."

The next year Dwight received an appointment as an official of the YMCA The clerk who inserted the Resolution of the Board of Managers put down for Dwight: "For the coming year at a salary of $_____."

The blank was never filled in because Dwight thought receiving a salary would hamper his newfound freedom from monetary restraint. He never again accepted a salary. In a year's time, his income went from roughly $5,000 to $150. He did it gladly in the name of Christ.

Having left the business world, Dwight poured himself with abandon into his mission Sunday school. He still had some financial resources from savings, but he spent freely on his "scholars" and on the school. He would fill his pockets with candy and other confections to entice the children to come to the school. He would also offer prizes such as a squirrel in a cage to the scholar who brought the most recruits in a given time. Nor did he ever fail to keep his promises to the children, and they knew they could trust him.

On the other hand, Dwight expected the children to keep their promises to him. One girl recalled: "If for some reason I broke my promise, I would sneak along the streets, in the hope of avoiding Mr. Moody and a reprimand. When I had almost reached home, he would stand before me with his hand outstretched and a sad look, and would greet me with, 'Why Jennie, where have you been? I missed you at Sabbath school. I hope you were not ill? Your folks are well? You will not disappoint me this coming Sabbath will you? It will make me very sad indeed if you fail me.' "

Dwight intensified his efforts to strengthen the school. He pressed his friends into a systematic slum visitation project. One of them, J. B. Stillson, reported, "We used to carry with us bread tickets, and a little money to relieve the sick, widows, and orphans, and had an arrangement with several physicians to visit the poor and sick without charge, and also to furnish the night watches."

Now that Dwight concentrated all his energy on the school, he became a whirlwind. People found it difficult, if not impossible to refuse the persistent Mr. Moody. A family living above a North Clark Street store soon encountered Dwight's persistence, which bordered on sheer stubbornness! The family's six children, recalled the store owner, were "noisy and ill-bred, and the father—who was a giant in size—was habitually drunk and violently abusive to his tiny wife. She supported the family by washing and scrubbing. Mr. Moody went again and again to try to convert the drunken father." Almost every day they would receive baskets of groceries, fruit, coal, or cordwood sent by Dwight.

Betsey Moody would have heartily endorsed her son's tireless battle against whiskey. Dwight, in keeping with the vow he had made to his mother, became a one-man crusade in his war on liquor. At one slum house, the father being absent, Dwight found, according to Farwell: "Not only children but a jug of whiskey. He took both out of the house: the children to his school, and the jug of whiskey to sprinkle the streets with." When Dwight next visited the home, the irate father shouted at him: "Did you pour away my whiskey?" As he took off his coat and rolled up his sleeves, he added, "I'll thrash you!"

Calmly, Dwight replied, "I broke the jug for the good of ourself and family. If I am to be thrashed, let me pray for you all before you do it."

But after the man listened to Dwight's heartfelt prayer

on the tenement floor, he felt ashamed and mumbled, "You had better just take the kids, not a whipping."

Dwight also exhibited a great deal of patience in waiting for his young students. He wasn't easily deterred. A small girl promised she would take Dwight home to get her mother's consent to come to the Sunday school. But she told him she had an errand to run first and asked him to wait on the street corner.

Dwight waited and waited—at least three hours—but still no sign of the girl. A few days later, he caught sight of her—and she saw him. She ran. He chased her as she ran over the raised plank sidewalks, clattering down and up the steps where the levels varied, dodging horse-drawn trams, and scattering dogs and old ladies, until finally she dashed through an alley. But Dwight pursued her even as she ran into a saloon and up the stairs to a bedroom and under the bed. Dwight followed her, perspiring and breathless, and at last coaxed the young girl to come out from under the bed. Through his doggedness in pursuing the girl, the entire family came to the Lord.

John Farwell observed the dark circles that had developed under Dwight's eyes and decided to give him a pony to ride so that at least he wouldn't have to walk the considerable distances within the city. People often referred to Dwight at this time as "Crazy Moody," because of his stamina and single-mindedness in sharing Christ. He became a familiar figure as a young, twenty-five-year-old man, riding a small pony through the Chicago streets, his trousers in bootlegs, and a cap on his head.

Sometimes, Dwight had to exert tough discipline on his children. One boy made his teacher's life a misery and disrupted neighboring classes. Finally, Dwight told Farwell, "I am going to take that boy into the police office below and whip him, and when you see me start for him have the school rise and sing the loudest hymn in the book until I return." Farwell did as he was told, and when Dwight returned, his face was very red from this "religious exercise." A month later, the boy became a Christian and proved to be a great help to his teachers.

Dwight's reputation in and around Chicago grew quickly. People considered him a "children's missionary." When some Irish Catholic boys broke some windows in the Mission Hall and beat up the scholars in the streets, Dwight decided it was time to take action. So he went to see the Roman Catholic bishop, the well-known James Duggan. Dwight persuaded the bishop to pray with him, and soon the trouble over the windows was resolved.

Another time, Dwight worked to get a young saloon keeper's son involved in the school. As he recalled: "I had never been in a saloon in my life. I walked by the door about a dozen times. I said, 'I can't go in there. People will think that I have come to get a drink.' " Then, as he looked in every direction and didn't see anyone from the church, he dashed in. The old father was behind the bar, and Dwight told him what he had come for. Later Dwight recalled that the father replied: "'We won't have any canting hypocrites here,' so I went back out quickly. But I tried a second time, and again he drove me out. On the third try, the old man wasn't quite so drunk or quite so cross, but he said he would rather have his sons drunkards and his daughters harlots than Christians."

But when Dwight discovered that the man edited a small rationalist newsletter, he promised to read Thomas Paine's *The Age of Reason* in return for the man's promise to read the New Testament.

One Sunday morning, Dwight saw an opportunity, so he said to the man, "I wish you would come to church with me."

The man retorted: "I haven't been to church in eighteen years. No, I won't go. But you may have a church here if you want to."

Appalled, Dwight thought, *A church in a saloon?* However, it seemed the only way to reach the man. Afraid of the church officers' disapproval, Dwight scheduled the service for a time when the regular church services were being held.

Then the man said, "I want you to understand, young man, that you are not going to do all the preaching."

"What do you mean?"

The man clarified his remark by saying, "I may want to say something, and my friends may want to say a word. We won't let you preach all the time. We may want to answer back."

So it happened that the atheists would speak forty-!five minutes, and Dwight only fifteen. Actually, Dwight wasn't sure he could preach more than fifteen minutes! Word got around about the meeting, and soon the place had to be moved because of the large number of skeptics attending. Dwight simply brought one small boy with him. But as he said, "He was one of my 'best' boys."

Describing the meeting, Dwight said, "They began to poke questions at me, but I said, 'No sir. You have got to preach forty-five minutes.' " Which they did, until Dwight was "sick and tired of infidelity." Then he quietly invited them to join him as he said, "Let us pray."

All the while Dwight prayed, they protested, jeered and sneered. Then he introduced his "secret weapon," the small boy who had come with him. The boy prayed "with a pleading voice and asked God to forgive these men for talking so against his dear Son." Each of the men began to steal away. Finally, the old saloon keeper said, "If that is what you teach your children, you may have mine."

Dwight rejoiced in the steady growth of the school. Now that he no longer "got the children for one hour in the week while the devil had them for the rest," he sensed God's peace about the situation. He wrote to his family, "I have been holding meetings in my school every night this winter. It has taken all of my time."

Seated on the platform, his eyes looking out over the crowd of dirty, ragged scholars, Dwight had no doubt that he had found his life's work and that he would be consumed within the city of Chicago, serving the children of the slums for the rest of his life.

Dwight little suspected the turn his life was about to take.

seven

War Efforts

O n Sunday, November 25, 1860, President-elect Abraham Lincoln visited Chicago. Through Farwell's invitation, he agreed to come to Moody's school provided they expected no speech. After attending church in the morning, he got to the mission at noon.

Mr. Lincoln sat through the opening prayers and hymns, then rose to leave. But Dwight boldly put Lincoln on the spot as he announced, "Mr. Lincoln has come to see the school on condition that he not be asked to speak. But if he wishes to say a word before leaving, we all have our ears open."

Lincoln made his way to the platform, then stopped, looked around, and said, "I was once as poor as any boy in the school, but I am now President of the United States, and if you attend to what is taught you here, some one of you may yet be President of the United States." Following some brief remarks, Mr. Lincoln marched out of the school.

Lincoln's short stay reminded Dwight of two strong opinions he held: he was an advocate for both the Union and abolition. Knowing little about the South, he considered most Southerners slave holders and felt that was wrong. He viewed the Civil War as a conflict between good and evil and would have been surprised to learn of the spiritual revival that swept through the Southern army.

After the firing on Fort Sumter, at least seventy-five members of Moody's school joined the army. Moody himself held a pacifist view similar to the Quakers, He stated: "I felt that I could not take a gun and shoot down a fellow human being. In this respect I am a Quaker." He also had the school to tend so dismissed any idea of going into the military.

Chicago, too, found itself much embroiled in the war, primarily through the erection of Camp Douglas, a military city of tents, barrack huts, parade grounds, and guard rooms designed to mobilize and train the citizen army arriving in droves. The camp, located a few miles south of Chicago, soon exerted a certain amount of influence on Chicago. Dwight and his friend Benjamin Franklin Jacobs, a young real estate agent, were appointed by the fledgling Young Men's Christian Association to provide Christian ministry to the new troops.

So Dwight and Benjamin began regular services at Camp Douglas. The men from farms and small towns pouring into the camp seemed ripe for a spiritual harvest. After leading sheltered lives, they found themselves suddenly thrust into the midst of excitement, temptation, and the uncertainty of going into combat.

From the beginning, servicemen showed interest in the meetings, and the YMCA met the growing demand for hymnbooks and other religious material. Dwight and Benjamin were thrilled from the outset with the meetings and the response when hundreds were led to seek Christ. Each night, Dwight returned to his room with several packs of surrendered playing cards which he carefully stored in a corner of the YMCA rooms.

Writing to his mother, he gushed, "I am all taken up with this." Then to assuage his mother, Dwight assured her when she complained about his not writing her often: "I think of you as often as I ever did but if I could see you & tell you how the Lord is blessing me in my labors I think you would say God Bless you, go forward. I am drove more now than ever in my life." He still had the responsibilities of Sunday school conventions and his own school as well and seemed to be in perpetual motion.

As the war continued, however, and the casualties began to come back to Camp Douglas, Dwight realized more than ever the sacredness of each individual life. Each life mattered to God, and each person needed the gift and assurance of eternal life.

Another dilemma faced him. He could no longer rely completely on Jacobs or others who knew how to preach. Dwight had a burning desire himself each time he met a soldier to tell him of the power of Christ to save. He must conquer his shyness and fear of speaking to others! Then he could "talk with them about my Savior that seems so near me—Oh, what would life be without Christ?"

At every turn, he felt his lack, his inadequacy. When Dwight's banker friend, Mr. Reynolds, hosted a dinner for ministers and laymen in the summer of 1861, one of the guests saw clearly Dwight's "earnestness in seeking to lead persons to the Savior, and his intense thirst for the knowledge of the Bible; for the entire dinner time was taken by Mr. Moody in quoting verses and in asking the ministers to tell him 'What does this verse mean?' " His wasted student life had come back to haunt him.

Farwell called Camp Douglas Dwight's "kindergarten of training." His promotion was rapid, and in the autumn, he considered becoming chaplain, but declined after friends in Chicago begged him not to join the army.

In the midst of his whirl of activity, Dwight wrote to his brother Samuel in January 1862: "I have some 500 or 800 people that are dependent on me for their daily food & new ones coming all of the time. I keep a sadall horse to ride around with to hunt up the poore people with & then I have a man to waite on the folks as they come to my office." He continues somewhat wearily but with mild enthusiasm, "I have just raised money enough to erect a chapell for the soldiers at the camp 3 miles from the city. I hold a meetig down thare evry day & 2 in the city so you see I have 3 meetigs to atend to every day be side calling on the sick. And that is not all. I have to go into the countrey about every week to buy wood & provisions for the poore also coal wheet meal & corn."

He also shared with his brother in a rather sad tone, "I do not get 5 minuets a day to study so I have to talk just as it happens. I do not answer one letter out of 10 that I get—I cannot get time—it is 11 to 12 every night when I retire & am up in the morning at light. I wish you could come in some time about 1 to 3 o'clock in my office hours and see the people waiting to see me."

Letters such as this one reveal the nonstop dynamo Dwight had become. He tended to measure godliness in terms of ceaseless activity, not according to the time spent with God alone. Still in his mid-twenties, he advocated going to church as much as possible and attending prayer meetings frequently. His motto, a good one, sums up his philosophy: "Do all you can to make the world better than you found it. Do all you can for Christ and then you will make others happy."

In the spring of 1862 following the battle of Shiloh in Tennessee, the YMCA organized a trainload of doctors, nurses, medical students, and supplies to be sent to the front. Dwight accompanied the personnel and supplies. How his heart broke as he observed the casualties of war! He reported to a colleague: "I tell you you do not know how roughley the poore fellows are treated. I was on the battlefield before they had buried the dead; it was awful to see the dead laying around without being anyone to burrey them." Dwight's urgency to share Christ accelerated, especially in the light of war's catastrophes.

En route to the Tennessee front, he conducted a prayer meeting in one car of the speeding train while a group of men played cards in an adjacent one! In the midst of wounded and dying men, Dwight witnessed the shattered limbs, the gangrene, the amputations often performed without chloroform, the deaths, and his heart ached. But he knew the urgent message he had to give these men who faced constant death was that of receiving Christ. Repeatedly, he asked them, "Are you a Christian?" When they answered affirmatively, Dwight knew he was in the Lord's will.

Accompanying over four hundred and fifty wounded men on a Tennessee River boat, Dwight and his companions "made up our minds we would not let a man die on the boat without telling him of Christ and Heaven—we would tell them of Christ as we gave them a cup of cold water."

The war deeply affected Dwight, but he had some unfinished business with Emma Revell. The man she had originally fallen in love with was a prosperous shoe salesman; now that same man had become a children's missionary and a preacher-at-large. Although Emma wondered where it would all end, she and Dwight were married in Chicago on Thursday, August 28, 1862. She was nineteen, and Dwight was twenty-five. After going "away on my weding tower," as Dwight expressed it, he and Emma moved into a tiny house on Chicago's North Side.

Emma, ever the virtuous wife, set about most subtly to "tame" Dwight. She saw the potential in Dwight—what he could become given some slight adjustments! One of the first things she did was to throw away Dwight's favorite patent shirts. He had boasted that he didn't need to wash them for weeks on end! For the time being, she failed in making him eat regular or adequate meals. One of Emma's greatest assets, however, was that she remained unflustered by the constantly changing events that whirled around Dwight. Dwight praised her in later years as the perfect companion: "She was the only one who never tried to hold me back from anything I wanted to do and was always in sympathy with every new venture."

Even married life failed to slow Dwight down. When brother Samuel came for a brief stay in the hopes of finding work, he noted, "Dwight is run from morning to night. He hardly gets time to eat. Camp Douglas is situated here (there is about 17,000), he holds meetings down there most every night—it is a treat to go down there and hear the soldiers sing, which is about 300 or 400 gathered from most every state." Samuel merely smiled when Dwight talked about religion, but Dwight kept praying for his entire family to come to the Savior.

Going to the war front at least nine times, Dwight ministered to multitudes of soldiers. He was under fire in January 1863, and among the wounded at the battle of Murfreesboro, Tennessee, as Rosecrans pushed toward Nashville. As he ministered, Dwight watched the dying find peace, until the certainty drilled into his consciousness that a person can know immediate, assured salvation.

"Chaplain, help me to die," whispered a casualty of Murfreesboro in the early morning hours. "I've been fighting Christ all my life. I had a praying mother, and I disregarded her prayers always."

Dwight read promise after promise from Scripture, "but he could not see them and I got nearly discouraged." Then Dwight began to read the story of Nicodemus from the Gospel of John. As he read, Dwight noted, "[the boy's] eyes became riveted upon me, and he seemed to drink in every syllable." Dwight came to the passage, "'And as Moses lifted up the serpent in the wilderness, even so must the Son of man be lifted up: that whosoever believeth in him should not perish, but have eternal life.' "

The soldier interrupted weakly, "What's that? Is that true? I want you just to read that again. . .That's good! Won't you read it again?"

So Dwight read the passage a second and then a third time, and in the flickering candlelight, he glimpsed the soldier's troubled face give way to a peaceful smile. As he stood by the empty cot the next morning, the orderly informed Dwight that the soldier had died restfully, murmuring the words of promise.

Spending much of his time moving in and around the wounded men, Dwight had a firsthand opportunity to minister and share his faith with them. Primarily, Dwight seemed to be acutely tuned to the heart needs of the sick and wounded men. More and more he would be invited to speak at gatherings, as well.

His experiences in the war vastly changed Dwight. Gone was the diffident, self-conscious amateur; by the fourth year, he had become a practiced, if homespun, preacher. In the spring of 1864, Major General Oliver Otis Howard, one of the Union generals, wrote of Dwight's effectiveness: "I was bringing together my Fourth Army Corps. Two divisions had already arrived and were encamped in and near Cleveland [Tennessee]. Our soldiers were just about to set out on what we all felt promised to be a hard and bloody campaign, and I think we were especially desirous of strong preaching. Crowds and crowds turned out to hear Moody. He showed them how a soldier could give his heart to God." Howard then gives his estimate of Dwight's preaching: "His preaching was direct and effective, and multitudes responded with a promise to follow Christ."

One of the soldiers who attended the meetings said that he "was much impressed with [Dwight's] earnestness. I wasn't at the time a Christian, though the thought had come to me that it would be well to begin the Atlanta campaign a soldier of Christ as well as a soldier of my country." After hearing the message one particular evening, "I went to my dog tent, opened a little copy of the New Testament, and began to read and pray my way into the kingdom of Christ. The joy of salvation came to me after a few days. I have always looked on Mr. Moody as my spiritual father."

As this company of soldiers left to fight in the Atlanta campaign and the March to the Sea, Dwight Moody returned to Chicago to some campaigns of another kind. However, he returned a much different individual than the haphazard minister who had left. He had acquired some poise and polish, but more than that, he understood what God required of him: to reach the souls of men.

eight

The Builder

Returning to Chicago, Dwight found his work cut out for him. The war had brought disruption to his Sunday school mission work and part of the North Market Hall where they met had burned in the fall of 1862.

When Dwight transferred his Sunday school to the dilapidated Kinzie Hall, enrollment went down. So once more, he set out to bring students in.

He never tired of thinking up new gimmicks and ways to lure boys and girls to the mission. This time, he picked a dozen or so of the most ragged-looking boys he could find, their names reflecting their individuality: Smikes, Madden the Butcher, Darby the Cobbler, Jackey Candles, and Black Stove Pipe. Dwight promised a new suit to each one who attended every Sunday until Christmas.

Dwight organized them into a class under John Farwell, and he deemed the boys "Moody's Bodyguard." He had the boys' picture taken before and after the issue of their new outfits. He captioned the before photo "Does It Pay?" The after photo stated: "It Does Pay." All except one of the boys earned his new suit of clothes—a fact that made Dwight proud.

But he began to have doubts about bribery. His City Relief Society was fooled too often. He shared with a colleague: "I have come to the conclusion that a loaf of bread in one hand and the Gospel in the other is wrong." However, the succor of the sick and destitute continued to have priority with Dwight in his work. He had little patience with those who preached bliss in heaven while doing little to alleviate misery on earth.

Another way Dwight used to interest students in Sunday school was his picnics, and he became well known for those alone. He himself loved contests and games of skill. Farwell only attended one picnic because he claimed that "the physical exercise to keep up with Mr. Moody in a race was too much for me." An assistant at the picnics recalled that "few at the picnics were his equal in racing, jumping, or other sports."

His practical jokes were also well known, and if a person could best Dwight in a joke, he was highly regarded, although this reversal seldom happened. When some of his teachers wanted to swim in the lake during a picnic, it was necessary to cross through a muddy bog. Dwight spoke to one young man dressed in fine clothes: "Mr. C. you get on my back and I will carry you across." Everything went well until they reached the middle of the swamp. Dwight dumped Mr. C., complete with white vest and lavender pants, into the muddy water, and Mr. C. had to manage as best he could to reach shore.

Dwight especially enjoyed jokes with a cruel barb even to the end of his life. His son, Paul, recalled: "While the tenderest-hearted man in the world, he would enjoy laughing at something the victim did not consider so excruciatingly funny. When I was a teenager, I got into a swarm of bees and was being stung numerous times.

Worse than the stings of the bees was the sight of my father actually rolling on the ground with laughter, but at a safe distance." This episode bears out the truth in a Moody family proverb: "No Moody ever laughs at anything unless blood is drawn."

By December 26, 1863, Emma wrote to Dwight's brother Sam that the new Sunday school building was almost completed. She said they hoped to be in the building within a few weeks; she affirmed the tremendous need for the new building and mentioned a roster of several prominent clergymen from different cities who would come to preach.

The new building, the very first to be owned by the Mission School, was built on Illinois Street between La Salle and Wells Streets at a cost of twenty-four thousand dollars. Underwritten by several wealthy patrons and with lesser amounts donated from parents and scholars, the building was completely paid for when it opened in the early months of 1864.

People commented on the building's odd shape calling it "a queer-looking brick building" with some semblance to a church. Someone else noticed that "houses crowd it in on either side so as to scarcely leave room for it to stand upon. It looks almost as if pains had been taken to make it as plain as possible so that no one, however poor, might be driven away by any outward display."

A huge gilded sign appeared on the right side of the entrance: EVER WELCOME TO THIS HOUSE OF GOD ARE STRANGERS AND THE POOR; a smaller sign read: THE SEATS ARE FREE. On the inside, various Scripture texts were posted in strategic places on the wall. The wall behind the platform, for example, had GOD IS LOVE affixed to it.

A visitor to the new building enjoyed what could have been called the school song: "Do You Know Any Little Barefoot Boy?" a song which evoked the very atmosphere and tone of the school:

> *Go bring him in, there is room to spare,*
> *Here are food and shelter and pity;*
> *And we'll not shut the door*
> *'Gainst one of Christ's poor*
> *Though you bring every child in the city.*

While listening to the song, the visitor looked down and "noticed most of the boys and girls were poor-looking, some barefoot, and most of the teachers seemed to be well dressed and altogether different from the scholars, and I said to myself 'Well, there isn't much looking after money here. They won't get much pay for looking after those boys and girls,' and I made up my mind I would come again. It wasn't long before I put my hand in Jesus Christ's hand, where it has been ever since."

Asking a small boy why he walked three miles every week to Illinois Street when there was a school near his home, Farwell was surprised to hear: "They love a fellow over here."

When Dwight's school had met in the North Market Hall, Dwight always urged the new converts to find city churches to join. But some of the poorer people tended to feel out of place in the more beautiful church buildings. And now that the mission had its very own building, many of these individuals wished to see the mission become an independent church.

The gathering of a new church was neither unusual nor difficult under Congregational custom. But Dwight hesitated. His mission was not Congregationalist, but united, its one formal link being to the YMCA. He frequently repeated, "If I thought I had one drop of sectarian blood in my constitution, I would open a vein and let it out."

The pressure from the converts mounted toward Dwight to form a church. Otherwise, they said, they would be sheep scattered and unfed.

Finally, Dwight gave in. A church was formed, and the official Manual of Illinois Street Church, printed in 1867, reads: "All were agreed that the church must be independent of all denominational connection, since those already gathered in the work represented nearly every evangelical denomination. It was therefore voted that the church be an Independent Church." Dwight and two friends drew up a simple doctrinal statement and articles of organization based on Congregationalist custom. At Emma's request, a baptistry along with a baptismal font were installed to accommodate both adult and infant baptism.

At first, Dwight invited students from the nearby Chicago Theological Seminary, a Congregationalist Seminary, to fill the pulpit. One Sunday, when the designated student failed to show up, Dwight himself had to preach. Farwell called it "providential."

Talking with children never seemed a problem for Dwight, but when it came to grownups, he thought he needed to switch gears and would try to imitate other preachers of the day. On one occasion, a minister looking for Dwight "found him in his room trying to get up a sermon. He had thrown off his coat and was struggling with his Bible and a concordance, while the sweat ran down his face."

About this same time, Dwight wondered if he should be ordained as a Congregationalist minister. The Chicago Seminary wanted to ordain him, especially since the Illinois Street Mission had become an independent church. Dwight asked his friend G. S. F. Savage what he thought about his being ordained. His friend replied: "Don't. If you are ordained you will be on the level with the rest of us. Now you are a preaching layman and that gives you an advantage. You are on the right road; keep to it." With that advice, Dwight declined ordination.

His very inadequacies and lack of proper grammar continued to drive him toward bettering himself. In 1865 he enrolled as a student in the newly formed Baptist Theological Seminary. How many lectures he attended is obscure; he did not proceed and was never ordained. If Dwight had been ordained in one denomination, he probably would not have drawn broad support from ministers in other denominations.

Dwight remained a lay pastor at the Illinois Street Independent Church until 1866 when a young seminary graduate was ordained to be minister. Dwight retained the title of superintendent—and effective control.

Still trying to conform to the ecclesiastical image of the day, Dwight's sermons tended to be clerical, his tone strident, and his themes evocative of fire and brimstone. So pronounced were his depictions of divine judgment,

Emma said she cringed when listening to them.

When ministering only to children, Dwight had not had to face man's degradation as much as he had later. Dealing with people of all ages, he saw human nature at its worst and reacted in the fashion typical of mission preachers of his day. He unabashedly confessed: "I preached that God hated sinners; that he was standing behind sinners with a double-edged sword ready to cut their heads off."

Dwight seemed to be two different people. From the pulpit he pounded and preached the wrath of God in the tradition of the old camp meetings. But in his basic personality at home, he remained genial, buoyant, bubbling with love and merriment.

One of the Illinois Street Church deacons, Watts de Golyer, tells of visiting the Moody home: "It was not an infrequent occurrence to hear peals of laughter over some joke administered mainly by the host, or somebody trying to get even with him. I remember a rule adopted and passed by himself that any person failing to hang up his hat or coat on the rack would find it in the yard. Shortly afterwards, I was busily employed finding and separating my belongings in the yard."

The birth of the Moody's first child, Emma Reynolds, on October 24, 1864, had contributed much to the joy and happiness in the Moody household. Dwight expressed his delight upon realizing that "both of her little fingers are as crooked as mine." Writing to his mother, he gushed: "They all say she looks like me but I must say I cannot see any resemblance."

However, Emma had no difficulty in seeing it. In some distress, she confided to a friend regarding little Emma when she was two: "She is so full of mischief. You would certainly think she was a second edition of D. L. Moody in his childhood." Despite her mischievous streak, Emma soon became the darling of her parents' hearts.

nine

Trying Times

As Dwight tried to settle back into some sort of routine following the war's end, he became more involved with the work of the YMCA. At the noon prayer meetings, Dwight was always on hand to greet everyone who entered. His enthusiasm and friendliness and genuine sincerity never failed to touch people.

A young man attending commercial school was "miserable, lonesome and homesick in the great city amid its great throngs who passed me by in restless haste and left me alone. Even in my boardinghouse no attention was paid to me. In my desperate loneliness I dropped into the noonday meetings. There Mr. Moody was first to grasp my hand and inquire all about me."

Prayer requests would come in from all over the city and would be read by the day's leader. Often upon hearing a request, Dwight would weep like a child in empathy. In him lay always something of the impressionable child, never far from tears, never far from laughter. Someone remarked after one of the noonday meetings: "Mr. D. L. Moody is so earnest, aggressive, and regardless of all namby-pamby notions of propriety in his work that he occasionally shocks the exceedingly proper people. At other times he is known to betray them into a laugh, a veritable guffaw right in prayer meeting."

His boundless energy was known and appreciated all over the city of Chicago, and in 1866, when a prominent businessman turned down the presidency of the Chicago Association (YMCA), he nominated Dwight Moody. Of course, Dwight had his detractors, too. Some said he was "too radical." Nevertheless, Dwight received the presidency at that time.

Too radical or not, Dwight was soon "on the warpath securing subscriptions"—as they described the energy with which he badgered the worthy and wealthy of the city. He reveled in turning the dollars of the rich into an institution which should, in a favorite phrase, "do good."

Two of the wealthy businessmen who contributed to this venture were Cyrus McCormick, inventor of the combine harvester, and George Armour, the meat packinghouse entrepreneur. Dwight and Emma became good friends with the McCormicks and were frequent guests at the millionaire's mansion.

Becoming known for his bold faith, Dwight often experienced astounding answers to prayer. One day, he rushed into the study of a Chicago minister with a sealed envelope. "Open that!" he cried. "Open it! There is a check for two thousand dollars in there."

"Are you sure? Have you seen it?"

"No. But I asked the Lord for it, and I know it's there! I came all the way across Chicago that you might prove my faith in prayer."

As the minister tore open the envelope, he discovered there was a two-thousand-dollar check inside, payable to the order of D. L. Moody and signed by Cyrus H. McCormick.

Dwight shared his story with the minister. He had gone to the millionaire, stating, "Mr. McCormick, the mission school is in dreadful straits!"

"Why you are striking me rather hard of late. I gave you something not long ago."

"I want a thousand."

"A thousand! Why surely you don't mean that, after all I've given you of late?" In any event Mr. McCormick agreed to make a donation. He went upstairs to write out a check.

"Just then," Dwight continued, "I thought to myself what a fool I was not to ask for two thousand! And I fell on my knees there in the parlor, and asked for two thousand. Mr. McCormick came downstairs with this sealed envelope. I thanked him and rushed over to you. Isn't my faith confirmed?"

The old minister was so curious as to what happened that he went to Mr. McCormick. "Can you recall the inducements or influences acting on your mind leading you to make the check for twice the amount asked for?"

Mr. McCormick thought for a moment, then replied: "Well, as I remember, I went upstairs to my desk and took out my checkbook. I wrote in 'D. L. Moody,' and then I began to think of the noble work he is doing in our city, and what a splendid fellow he is. Finally I concluded to make the check for the amount I did."

Dwight told the minister's son sometime later that "God gave me the money that day because I needed it. And He has always given me money when I needed it. But often I have asked Him when I thought I needed it, and He has said, 'No, Moody, you just shin along the best way you can. It'll do you good to be hard up awhile.' "

Although Cyrus McCormick thought well of Dwight, Chicago's respectful estimate of him had dissolved since the war. "He was often most brutally ridiculed and buffeted and persecuted," recalled an acquaintance. "His language, his looks, his methods of work were made objects of ridicule and burlesque, and the most cruel remarks were passed from mouth to mouth about him."

A Chicago journalist who had no use for Dwight criticized his "early excrescences of manner." He added that "the established pulpit, especially in its higher or formal ranges, contended that he lowered religion." And the man on the street spoke of Dwight's always being on the go, "except when he might halt a stranger anywhere, to interrogate him on the state of his soul; and even when his amazed or abashed victim was gathering his wits to frame an answer suited to the astonishing occasion, off he would be to startle somebody else into 'fits of salvation.' "

Dwight had made a vow to God not to pass a day without speaking to someone about Christ. His stock question to everyone became, "Are you a Christian?" He shouted this question from the platform, he whispered it in the narrow passageway, he asked it to his dinner-table companions. Wherever he happened to be, Dwight was sure to confront everyone nearby with this question.

When he saw a man leaning up against a lamppost, Dwight approached him and said, "Are you a Christian?" The man responded with damnation and curses and told him to mind his own business. Later, the man told a mutual friend that he had never been so insulted. Three months later, Dwight was awakened in the middle of the night. At the door "stood this stranger I had made so mad at the lamppost," to confess that he had known no peace. "Oh, tell me what to do to be saved!"

Dwight's close friends winced with him from the ridicule, and Farwell even suggested that he was doing more harm than good when he shouted at people at every turn. Dwight replied calmly, "You are not my boss. God is my boss."

Heckled in the stockyards and subjected to catcalls outside the courthouse, Dwight remained undaunted in his one-man mission. After one brutish episode, a young doctor in the crowd who was impressed by the preacher's "dauntless manner," asked who he was. A bystander glanced at the inquirer with some disdain and responded, "Why, that's Moody!"

These were the years when Dwight's nickname became "Crazy Moody." He drove himself mercilessly, paying little attention to Emma who urged him to eat regular meals. He admitted later that, "I was an older man before thirty than I have been since." Despite his frenzied, sometimes obnoxious ways to win others to Christ, Dwight's humility redeemed him. He always showed a willingness to listen, to learn, to experiment, and he possessed a basic common sense, which helped him immeasurably. His burning desire as far back as he could remember was "that every soul be saved."

Although Dwight was willing to continue working in Chicago, his wife's health changed his mind. The Moodys decided to sail to England because of Emma's asthma. This trip started Dwight Moody in new directions.

ten

Going Abroad

Occasionally in his rare quiet moments, Dwight had thought about visiting England. He felt his spiritual and mental needs keenly. But he moved much too fast in Chicago to address them.

Dwight greatly admired and desired to meet three individuals in England: George Williams, founder of the YMCA and a London wholesale draper; George Muller of Bristol, the elderly German who prayed and, without capital or asking anyone for a penny, maintained a large orphanage and numerous overseas missionaries; and Charles Haddon Spurgeon, Dwight's senior by only three years, yet a preacher of fame and like himself virtually self-taught, jovial, and rather stout.

Spurgeon's sermons preached from the Metropolitan Tabernacle, his Baptist church in South London, were spread worldwide—their homespun language, anecdotes, humor, grasp of Scripture, all made Dwight eager to imitate this great man of God. Dwight read everything he could find of Spurgeon's.

Much as he desired to travel to England, Dwight would never have gone had Emma's doctor not suggested it for her asthma. Mrs. Revell gladly kept baby Emma, and Dwight and Emma set sail for England on February 24, 1867, shortly after Dwight's thirtieth birthday.

Emma loved the sea voyage, but poor Dwight suffered from seasickness the entire trip! Shortly after their arrival, Dwight still recovering, said, "One trip across the water is enough for me"; then he added, "I do not expect to visit this country again." Both statements turned out to be totally false.

The couple's first impressions of England left something to be desired. It either snowed or rained most of their first week. Dwight disliked the British formality and wrote his mother: "I do not like the old country as well as our one, I must tell you how glad I am I was born and brought up in America. I think England must be a horrible place to live."

Although a born Londoner, Emma agreed completely with her husband. She considered London as sooty as Pittsburgh; the Bank of England timeworn; and St. Paul's Cathedral "a very grand building but more appropriate for any other kind of performance than for a church service!"

Making their way the following Sunday to the Metropolitan Tabernacle, Spurgeon's church, Dwight marveled at the huge congregation of at least five thousand. He remarked to Emma later, "When Spurgeon walked to the platform, my eyes just feasted upon him, and my heart's desire for years has at last been accomplished!" It seemed to Dwight like a dream come true, to be listening to Spurgeon after all the time he had admired him. Silently Dwight prayed, "Oh, Lord, help me to preach and minister like Charles Spurgeon! I pray for grace and to be filled with the Holy Spirit to minister to Your people."

Emma described Spurgeon: "He is a very plain-looking man but had the undivided attention of his whole audience—and the singing—so many voices mingled together in such harmony and keeping such good time, it seemed perfectly grand!" How Dwight longed to preach as Spurgeon preached and to see singing led like that. His heart nearly burst at the thought of such a possibility.

In London, Dwight met George Williams and received an invitation to the annual breakfast of the original YMCA in Aldersgate Street; he encouraged them to start a daily noon prayer meeting similar to the one in Chicago. The meeting flourished, continuing without interruption until World War I.

As time passed and spring came on, the Moodys were invited to various social gatherings, and their perception of England began to change. Emma thought London prettier in the springtime and "some of the parks and square gardens are extremely beautiful." And, she told Dwight that she "liked the English better than when I first came. I do not think them as reserved as I expected them, but do not think them as free and open as Americans."

Dwight enjoyed the sensation of being appreciated. In Chicago, he recalled, Episcopalians would pass by on the other side of the street or call him names. But in England, the Church of England clergy and laymen he met were kind to him. Evangelicals, both Anglican and nonconformist, took to him.

Of course, Dwight appeared somewhat of a novelty to the British. His expansive geniality, his sincerity and drive caused a religious newspaper to declare, "How deeply and quickly Dwight L. Moody has won the affections of a multitude of Christian brethren." Dwight relished the new attention, and his estimation of the British climbed because they received him so openly.

Dwight received an invitation to address the May meeting of the Sunday School Union in London. The meeting took place at Exeter Hall in the Strand, long considered the Mecca of Evangelicals. Lord Shaftes-bury, the well-known philanthropist and leading abolitionist, introduced Dwight by saying, "We are very glad to welcome our American cousin, the Reverend Mr. Moody of Chicago."

Dwight stood up. He gazed at the stern-looking godly faces, the ladies' prim bonnets and crinolines, the whiskers and formal black of the men; they were all drowsy and satiated with speeches on a warm May afternoon, and most likely they considered an American a sort of colonial who was not quite English and had a vulgar, grating accent.

Every eye riveted on him, Dwight said: "The vice-chairman has made two mistakes." He had the audience's attention as they sat bolt upright. "To begin with, I'm not 'the Reverend Mr. Moody' at all. I'm plain Dwight L. Moody, a Sabbath school worker. And then I'm not your American cousin. By the grace of God I'm your brother, interested with you in our Father's work for His children."

Dwight paused, then with a slight grin, added, "And now about this vote of thanks to the 'noble Earl.' I don't see why we should thank him any more than he should thank us."

The audience gasped, but then as they observed Lord

Shaftesbury, who possessed a great sense of humor and lacked any pomposity, they relaxed and delighted in the American's frankness. Once the air had been cleared, Dwight urged the audience to have done with colorless catechisms and tedious verselearning and to act on the belief that children could trust in Christ as a friend.

Some of the interesting people Dwight met in England had a lasting impact on him. One of them was a wholesale butcher in West London, Henry Varley. Varley, close to Dwight's age, belonged to the Plymouth Brethren group. His preaching, however, was remarkable; he preached with such force that several hundred people would gather to hear him.

Dwight, curious about Varley's power, visited him to discover his secret of success. Varley believed in much prayer, so he prayed at home. Then, as they took a small carriage over the rough stone streets of London, he said, "Now, brother, let us have prayer for the meeting," and he knelt on the swaying carriage floor, among the wisps of straw.

Dwight had never tried praying aloud in a carriage as it swayed back and forth and rumbled along over the cobblestone streets. In fact, it wasn't exactly a comfortable or convenient place to pray! But following the evening service, he watched spellbound as seventy butchers with tears streaming down their faces gathered around Varley, truly a man of God. Dwight knew that prayer was Varley's secret.

At Varley's invitation, Dwight received several opportunities to preach, which he gladly fulfilled. At the close of a service he preached in Dublin, he heard someone speak at his shoulder level: "Ah'm 'Arry Moorhouse. Ah'll coom and preach for you in Chicago."

Dwight turned around. Just in front of him stood a beardless, insignificant-looking, small man. He appeared to be about seventeen years old. Slightly annoyed, yet attempting to hide his disdain, Dwight smiled a benevolent smile. Not to be put off, the little fellow repeated, "Ah'm 'Arry Moorhouse. Ah'll preach for you in America. When d'you go 'ome?"

Now Dwight felt cornered and hedged a bit, "I'm not quite sure when we'll leave. Things are quite unsettled for me and my wife just now." If Dwight had known his departure date, he wasn't sure that he would have revealed it to this odd, little character anyway.

Harry Moorhouse's name had been mentioned to Dwight, and he knew a few things about him. God had retrieved Harry from the gutter—and from picking pockets. Although Harry was known as the "Boy Preacher," Dwight found it hard to believe this mere stripling of a lad could preach and soon forgot all about him.

Not long after the encounter with Moorhouse, Dwight and Emma returned to Chicago and were thankful to be home. Much to their surprise and delight, a home had been built for them on State Street and given to them as a gift. Their friend John Farwell had asked other friends of the Moodys to help purchase and furnish the house. Two portraits of Dwight and Emma had also been placed prominently in the new house. G. P. A. Healy, the most famous American portrait painter of the day, had painted Dwight's portrait without fee.

The opening of the new YMCA hall on Madison Street provided the Moodys with further excitement. Designed by W. W. Boyington, an outstanding architect in the area, the hall had been erected in the center of Chicago's business district. The first building in the world to be built by a YMCA, the hall rose five stories, had a marble façade, the largest auditorium in Chicago, five shops to lease at street level, a library, reading room, lecture rooms, a gymnasium, a dormitory for forty-two people, and extra office space rented by the fire, police, and health departments.

Officials of the YMCA had intended to name the new hall Moody Hall, but Dwight demurred and insisted it be called Farwell Hall in honor of John Farwell. Everyone knew, however, that the new YMCA represented Dwight's crowning achievement in Chicago. They realized, too, that Dwight was one of their leading citizens, albeit a somewhat abused one.

A description of him appeared in a local religious newspaper in November 1867: "Mr. Moody is rather below the medium height, and inclined to fleshiness, not corpulence. He goes to the platform with a quick, nervous step that means business; and behind his round, ruddy and good-humored but earnest face is a busy brain." The newspaper account attached some further accolades to Dwight: "When Moody speaks, everybody listens, even those who don't like him. His remarks are short, pithy and practical, and his exhortations impressive and sometimes touching even to tears. He is aggressive and his remarks always have a martial ring." The account said nothing about his being ill-educated, although it did refer to his being short—he appeared shorter because he had gained considerable weight, a fact which concerned Dwight but one he could not seem to control.

Just when Dwight thought his situation in Chicago couldn't get much better, he received an unexpected irritant in the form of a letter from Harry Moorhouse. The young man had arrived in New York and wanted to come to Chicago and preach for Dwight. Politely, Dwight dropped him a note saying, "If you come West, call on me." Dwight soon dismissed Moorhouse from his mind, thinking, *I'll never hear from him again.*

Twenty-seven-year-old Harry Moorhouse had served time in jail before his twenty-first birthday. After getting out, he came upon a back-street mission and heard an ex-prize fighter and coal miner preach on the Prodigal Son. Slowly, he began to be transformed even though he wore thick gloves at first to keep from picking pockets! He became a respectable auctioneer, married a childhood friend, then moved to a tiny cottage on the outskirts of Manchester to give his whole time to preaching.

A whimsical, gentle creature, and self-effacing, Moorhouse possessed a burning sense of mission. A strong sense of humor and an ability to prick the slightest bubble of pretension brought a wonderful balance to his life.

Upon arrival in New York, Moorhouse stayed in the home of a rich Quaker, William Kimber, who found himself quite taken with the young man. Kimber tried to help Moorhouse with his grammar, spending many hours using an accepted grammar book to help correct his errors. Kimber wished to enhance Moorhouse's "wonderful gospel messages" with proper grammar to make them more palatable.

Dwight, of course, knew nothing about William Kimber or of his helping Moorhouse with his grammar. If he thought at all of Moorhouse after January 1, 1868, he felt relief that he had heard the last of him.

But on January 7, even as Farwell Hall still glistened with new paint, fire broke out. No police, health, or fire department on the premises could save it from the strong winds that blew that day. A young boarder, David Borrell, had reached the doorway carrying his trunk when Dwight called, "Borrell, throw it away and help me. We want to have a prayer meeting in the Methodist Church." The noonday meeting took place, and even before the rubble cooled, the YMCA secretary and committee began soliciting for funds to rebuild the prestigious hall.

A few weeks after the fire, Dwight annoyingly heard from Moorhouse again. In his letter he told Dwight the date and time for his Chicago visit. Reading it with some impatience, Dwight thought, *The man can't preach!* Fortunately, from Dwight's perspective, he had to be in St. Louis for the Missouri Christian Convention the day of Moorhouse's arrival.

The day of Dwight's departure for St. Louis, he asked Emma to put Moorhouse up, then he told the deacons, "Try him—and if he fails I will take him off your hands when I come back." After which he boarded the train for St. Louis.

Dwight had been in demand in the Northwest as a convention speaker. His ability to draw ministers and lay people of differing denominations and viewpoints was considered valuable. The men in charge of these conventions knew Dwight to be a man who would stir sluggish saints, resolve differences, and bring about unity in the effort against unbelief, apostasy, and indifference. Materialism, too, was fast gaining ground across the nation, and multitudes were being caught up in its pursuit.

Speaking forcefully in an election year, Dwight emphasized, "We can carry this state and hold it for Christ. The power lies buried in the church, and the question is how to get it developed." As usual, he enjoyed a warm reception for his speech—and his conciliatory ideas.

Meanwhile, back in Chicago, Harry Moorhouse put in his appearance. Seventeen-year-old Fleming Revell, Jr. spending some time with his sister and brother-in-law, saw him first. He had expected someone long-bearded, stately, and dignified. Instead at the door stood a "little stripling, an insignificant-looking little Englishman who announced triumphantly, "I am 'Arry Moorhouse.' " Fleming asked him to repeat his name, which he did. Then Moorhouse asked with some bewilderment, "This is Mr. Moody's 'ouse, isn't it?" Receiving assurance, the little man toddled in!

With much misgiving that Thursday night, the deacons let Moorhouse preach at a small meeting in the basement. Even though they struggled to understand him and his message was very different from any they had heard, they agreed to have him preach again the following night.

When Dwight returned on Saturday, he asked Emma about Moorhouse. Much to his amazement, she replied, "They liked him very much. He preaches a little different from you. He preaches that God loves sinners!"

Dwight figured if someone preached differently from him, the other person was out of step. He looked with dread toward the next day because he knew he wouldn't care for Moorhouse's preaching!

eleven

Turning Points

On Sunday morning, Dwight found himself in a somewhat expectant mood. *Well, at least I haven't had to prepare a message today,* he thought. *I am tired from my trip. I just hope this Moorhouse fellow isn't too bad. But I can tolerate him for at least one message!*

Emma, with enthusiasm, reassured Dwight that, "Mr. Moorhouse backs up everything he says with the Bible. I think you will agree with him when you hear him preach."

Hearing a strange sound at the service, Dwight realized the people were all carrying Bibles. He had never told them that laypeople should bring Bibles, and it seemed odd to see the people coming in with Bibles and to listen to the flutter of Bible pages as the Scripture was announced.

Then the service began and Moorhouse declared his text: "John 3:16: 'God so loved the world that he gave his only begotten son, that whosoever believeth in him should not perish but have everlasting life.' " Instead of dividing the text into three parts in ministerial fashion, Moorhouse went from Genesis to Revelation, proving that God loves the sinner. Before he finished, Dwight noted that "he spoiled two or three of my sermons!"

Dwight's teaching that God hates the sinner as well as the sin suddenly lay in shambles at his feet. Admitting to a friend later, Dwight said, "I never knew up to that time that God loved us so much. This heart of mine began to thaw out; I could not keep back the tears."

Dwight's young brother-in-law, Fleming Revell observed Dwight that Sunday and "saw him just drinking in the message that Sunday morning, February 8, 1868. Then Sunday evening, little Harry Moorhouse stood swaying from one foot to another in his seeming awkwardness, but you forgot all about it as you heard the message coming from his lips." Again, Sunday night, Moorhouse used the same text and unfolded from Genesis to Revelation God's love for man. It was not so much a sermon as a Bible reading, consisting of a string of related texts or passages.

As Moorhouse concluded, Dwight jumped to his feet and announced: "Mr. Moorhouse will speak every night this week. Everybody come. Tell your friends to come!"

So it continued, night after night as Moorhouse spoke he reaffirmed the love of God for sinners. One night, he haltingly stated: "My friends, for a whole week I have been trying to tell you how much God loves you, but I cannot do it with this poor stammering tongue."

Gradually as the truth of Moorhouse's messages broke in on Dwight, he found himself being transformed into an apostle of love. No more would he preach the wrenchingly bitter and fearful sermons about God's hatred for man. How could he have so misunderstood God's Word? From then on, he would do his best to remedy whatever ills he had committed in his sermons.

During the daytime, Moorhouse enjoyed the place of honored guest in the Moody household. His little ways and comic sayings and Lancashire accent enhanced his charm, but more than those, he taught Dwight how to read and study the Bible.

Dwight had always looked on the Bible as a text-book—and as a weapon. German Higher Criticism had scarcely penetrated the theological world of Chicago, much less Dwight's world, so he was unaware of the critical problems and disputes that went on in some circles over the Bible. To him it was the Word of God, but he regarded it as an armory of well-worn texts on which to peg talks and sermons or to throw at individuals. He was curiously ignorant of much that the Bible taught.

Gently, Harry Moorhouse told Dwight that he didn't know his Bible; he showed him how to treat it as an entity and to trace the unfolding themes of Scripture. He helped him see that "it is God's Word, not our comment upon it, that saves souls." Above all, Moorhouse warned Dwight that he needed to take in more than he gave out. It wasn't long before Dwight rose very early in the morning while the rest of the household slept. He lit and trimmed the oil lamp in the study and poured for an hour or more over his big Bible, scribbling notes in the margin.

After Moorhouse left, Fleming Revell recorded in his diary that "D. L. Moody had great power before, but nothing like what he had after dear Harry Moorhouse came into our lives and changed the character of the teaching and preaching in the chapel."

Almost as a footnote, Dwight said in addressing the Illinois State Sunday School Convention at Du Quoin that same summer of 1868, "Be kind—conquer by love. If a man has his heart full of love and a little common sense, he will succeed."

The years of 1870-71 were ones of major change for Dwight. He had long realized the importance of song in gospel meetings. Although he himself was pretty much tone deaf and definitely not a singer, he could be powerfully impressed by a hymn. He saw that singing created a mood of worship and response, especially among the semilliterate poor; however, from his childhood background, he became suspicious about music such as oratorios and operatic renditions.

Dwight enjoyed conducting the singing during the meetings, using hymn singing as a weapon. "You sing over there!" he would call out. "Now you sing. Now you sing down there. And now everybody sing." When asked why he did this, Dwight replied earnestly, "They will forget what I say, but if they learn 'Jesus, Lover of My Soul,' and will sing it to themselves; they will get it in their mouths at least, and they will get the Gospel along with it!"

For a few years, Dwight had searched off and on for a song leader. Sometimes an older man, Philip Phillips, known as the "Pilgrim Singer," sang at Dwight's meetings. Phillips, unfortunately, did not live in Chicago.

Then in the summer of 1869, Dwight met another song leader, Philip Paul Bliss. Bliss was a lovable, cheerful man with beautiful manners and could write hymns that children and semilliterate people learned easily. Through Philip Bliss, Dwight's sense of the power of singing in gospel work crystallized.

Bliss helped Dwight on Sunday evenings when in Chicago, but by July, he was lured away to become choirmaster of the First Congregational Church. One outstanding gospel song that Bliss wrote while working with Dwight was "Hold the Fort: I Am Coming," based on the defense of Altoona during the Civil War's Atlanta Campaign. Sherman had signaled the message "Hold the Fort," in the presence of the fierce defense. But the message took on Christian connotations and became popular in America and Great Britain.

Later in July, Dwight attended the YMCA International Convention held in Indianapolis. One morning when leading an early prayer meeting, Dwight saw Ira David Sankey, a participant, arrive late and sit near the door. A fastidious, well-groomed man, Sankey had every hair of his handsome, muttonchop whiskers in place. A long-winded man droned on and on in prayer, and the others began to get restless. Sankey's neighbor, a Presbyterian minister, whispered, "The singing here has been abominable. I wish you would start up something when that man stops praying, if he ever does."

When the man quit, Sankey started "There Is a Fountain Filled with Blood." The congregation joined in, and the meeting continued forward.

Afterward, the minister introduced Sankey to Dwight. As was his custom, Dwight sized him up in a second.

"Where are you from? Are you married? What is your business?"

Sankey, taken aback, quickly responded, "New Castle, Pennsylvania. I am married, two children. In government service, revenue."

Dwight shot back, "You will have to give that up."

Sankey could scarcely believe his ears. He stood amazed and at a loss to understand why this man told him he would have to give up a good position.

"What for?" gasped Sankey.

"To come to Chicago to help me in my work."

Over Sankey's protest that he could not leave his business, Dwight insisted: "You must. I have been looking for you for the last eight years."

Sankey conceded finally to pray with Dwight briefly in the vestry but had no thought of giving up his position. He had just become aware only a day or two earlier while listening to someone else of the tremendous power in a simple gospel hymn when the singer put his whole heart and soul into it. The influence of the hymn had imparted to Sankey a great desire to use his own voice in a similar manner. He had not expected his desire to be fulfilled so quickly.

The following afternoon he received an urgent note requiring him to come to a street corner. As factory crowds left for home, Dwight told Sankey to get on a soapbox, a comedown of sorts for this handsome young man. Commanded to sing, Sankey proceeded, and a crowd gathered. As Dwight began to talk, more and more people came to hear him. Twenty-five minutes later, Dwight told the people they would continue in the Opera House rented by the YMCA International Convention. Sankey and his friends led the way singing, "Shall We Gather at the River."

Sankey left Indianapolis completely unsettled about the matter of joining Moody. In a tumult, he prayed, recalling later: "I presume I prayed one way, and he prayed another." It took just six months for Dwight to pray Sankey out of business!

Sankey had been born in Edinburg, Pennsylvania, on August 28, 1840. He had lived most of his life in a neighboring area, New Castle, and belonged to the Methodist Church.

Serving briefly in the Civil War, it was said that he owed his life to his voice. On sentry duty one night, he began to sing a favorite hymn when a Confederate sniper got him in his sights; the sniper was so moved by the singing that he lowered his rifle.

Consenting to a trial week with Dwight in 1871, Sankey resigned his job with the Civil Service. His wife agreed, despite never having lived so far from New Castle. So Sankey and Moody joined forces, but local buffs were not impressed. John Hitchcock called Sankey "a comparatively obscure man whose presence amongst us is not regarded in musical circles as a great acquisition to their forces." Time would prove him to be wrong.

The Moody whom Sankey joined was a man facing a dilemma. He stood at a crossroads in his life as postwar America vacillated between greed in the North and resentment in the South. The country had not yet come together in renewed unity following the war.

Of course, Dwight's energies remained undiminished and his zeal for men's souls unsurpassed, but he was uncertain about remaining in Chicago with the mission school, the church, and his other activities and commitments. And his popularity and demand as a speaker continued unabated.

In the summer of 1868, because of his success in Chicago's slums, a national convention held at the Marble Church in New York City extended an invitation to him. Some people objected to Dwight's name being on the roster with well-known preachers like Dr. John Hall and Henry Ward Beecher, but his address was well received. Someone at the meeting observed that Dwight "claimed attention at once, and I believe you could have heard a pin drop all through that hour. It seemed to me that he just grew larger and larger. Mr. Moody was a revelation to us on 'how to reach the masses.'"

Then there was the political maneuvering. . .when certain individuals wanted Dwight to run for Congress, for governor, and even for president! Dwight's response to all these ideas remained, "I have got a higher service than that!"

But where did God want him to be? He enjoyed his home, and while he had considered being an itinerant evangelist, he couldn't bear the thought of being gone so much of the time. He thrived on quick trips to this city or that for evangelistic-type forays but always looked forward to coming back home. Once little William Revell Moody put in his appearance on March 25, 1869, Dwight had even more reason not to stray too far from home.

Always uppermost in Dwight's mind was the plight of Chicago's poor. On a New Year's Day, John Hitchcock accompanied Dwight and the church officers as they called on two hundred families. Hitchcock remembered the day's hectic pace:

"On reaching a family belonging to his congregation, he

would spring out of the bus, lead up the stairways, rush into the room, and pay his respects: 'You know me: I am Moody; this is Deacon De Golyer, this is Deacon Thane, this is Brother Hitchcock. Are you all well? Do you all come to church and Sunday school? Have you all the coal you need for the winter? Let us pray.' And down we would go upon our knees, while Mr. Moody offered from fifteen to twenty words of earnest, tender sympathetic supplication that God would bless the man, his wife, and each of the children. Then, springing to his feet, he would dash on his hat, dart through the doorway and down the stairs throwing a hearty 'good-bye' behind him, leap into the bus, and off to the next place on his list; the entire exercise occupying about one minute and a half."

Hitchcock continues: "Before long the horses were tired out, for Moody insisted on their going at a run, so the omnibus was abandoned and the party proceeded on foot. One after another his companions became exhausted with running upstairs and downstairs and across the streets and kneeling on bare floors and getting up in a hurry; until the tireless pastor was left to make the last of the two hundred calls alone; after which feat he returned home in the highest spirits, and with no sense of fatigue, to laugh at his exhausted companions for deserting him."

As usual, ceaseless activity filled Dwight's days. Activities such as the tract campaign at the YMCA where the men carried over a million tracts to Chicago's inhabitants gratified him. He also participated in endless fund-raising to keep all the projects going and organized a "Yokefellows" group that would frequent saloons, boardinghouses, and street corners to bring people into Farwell Hall.

He had much detested office work as a result of these projects but tended to put it off. Eventually he was on ten or twelve committees, and the situation finally became critical. Sadly, Dwight realized, "My hands were full. If a man came to talk about his soul I would say: 'I haven't time: got a committee to attend.'"

Dwight knew his life had gotten much too complicated. His involvement in various activities used to satisfy him, but now he sensed an inner struggle. He knew God was calling him into a higher service, "to go out and preach the Gospel all over the land instead of staying in Chicago. I fought against it."

The tension building within Dwight spilled over into his preaching. He realized that his preaching was no longer as effective. The inner tension, the half-recognized rebellion against God's will, the tangled objectives, and the utter lack of integration combined to insure that Dwight's speaking and preaching were no longer like St. Paul's, "in demonstration of the Spirit and of power."

God began to intervene in Dwight's life through two women: Sarah Anne Cooke, an Englishwoman, and her widow friend, Mrs. Hawxhurst.

twelve

God's Fire

The first woman, Sarah Anne Cooke, had recently emigrated from England. Just ten years older than Dwight, she seemed wise in the ways of God and attended numerous religious meetings with regularity. A Free Methodist, Mrs. Cooke, as a friend described her, "Spoke only in the language of Zion, was full of good works, and buttonholed the unwary to exhort them to flee from the wrath to come."

Attending a camp meeting in June 1871, Mrs. Cooke said reverently that, "a burden came on me for Mr. Moody, that the Lord would give him the baptism of the Holy Ghost and of fire." Soon she solicited her friend Mrs. Hawxhurst, who was a widow, to pray with her.

The two women seated themselves in the front row of Dwight's church, and while he preached, they prayed.

After the service they would say to him, "We have been praying for you."

Unnerved, Dwight responded, "Why don't you pray for the people?"

The ladies: "Because you need the power of the Spirit."

Disgusted, Dwight muttered through his beard, "I need the power?"

They paid him no attention but just continued praying

and, as they had opportunity, speaking to him.

He resented them sitting in the front row, and it became increasingly difficult to preach. The women persisted. At first they found "little conviction of his need," but as they continued to pray, Dwight asked them to come to his home and talk with him.

While there, the ladies poured out their hearts in prayer, asking God to fill Dwight with the power of the Holy Spirit. Unexpectedly, a great hunger began to form in Dwight's soul. He said later, "I did not know what it was, and I began to cry out as I never did before. I really felt that I did not want to live if I could not have this power for service."

But the power would not come, perhaps because Dwight refused to heed the call "to go out all over the land."

In September Dwight invited Mrs. Cooke, whom he called "Auntie," and Mrs. Hawxhurst to pray with him each Friday afternoon in his room at Farwell Hall. They all prayed aloud in turn. On Friday, October 6, as Mrs. Cooke said later, "Mr. Moody's agony was so great that he rolled on the floor and in the midst of many tears and groans cried to God to be baptized with the Holy Ghost and with fire."

Silence reigned—the heavens were as brass with no answer forthcoming from heaven.

Dwight's inner struggle refused to resolve—he would not place himself on the altar, would not yield to God in his determination to stay in Chicago. How could he leave the thriving mission building in Illinois Street? Who else could hold sway in that great monument to his organizing zeal, Farwell Hall, with its two hundred gas jets, its monstrous reflectors, its seats for 2500, its splendid organ? Nothing should move him from these two dear buildings. . .but still Dwight heard the still small voice whispering to his spirit: "Go out and preach the Gospel all over the land." Surely God couldn't be telling him to leave everything he had worked for!

That Sunday evening, October 8, a capacity crowd filled Farwell Hall. Dwight's message went forth supercharged, and Sankey sang "Today the Savior Calls" like an angel. As Sankey reached the closing words of the third verse: "and death is nigh," the loud noise of fire engines rushing past the hall drowned out his voice. Then, the deep, sonorous tones of the great city bell in the old courthouse steeple pealed forth their warning alarm.

Confusion reigned in the street as people rushed by, and Dwight decided to close the meeting at once because of the audience's restlessness and growing anxiety.

As Dwight and Sankey sprinted out the back door, they glimpsed an angry red smudge in the southwest part of the sky. Immediately, they separated, Sankey to help at the scene, and Dwight to cross the river for home to reassure Emma and the children. As he hurried along, the southwest wind rose almost to hurricane force, and the sky became bright with a fireworks display as sparks blew and house after house caught fire from the hungry flames. Bursting into his house, Dwight cried out to Emma, "The city's doomed!"

By midnight the ravenous flames had engulfed much of Chicago. Crashing buildings, wild neighing of terrified horses, and shouts of firefighters and refugees combined in an ominous cacophony. Sankey ran back to Farwell

Hall, all the while shaking falling embers from his coat. Hastily, he grabbed a few of his belongings and headed for Lake Michigan.

The Moody home, temporarily thought to be secure, was quickly roused to action when police knocked on their door at midnight. As he speedily gathered some Bibles and a few valuables, Dwight arranged for a neighbor who owned a horse and buggy to take the children to friends in a northern suburb.

Emma begged Dwight to save the Healy portrait. Laughingly, Dwight exclaimed, "Take my own picture! That would be a joke. Suppose I meet some friends in the same trouble as ourselves and they say, 'Hullo, Moody, glad you have escaped. What's that you've saved and cling to so affectionately?' Wouldn't it sound great to reply, 'Oh, I've got my own portrait!' " Just then, looters entered their home, and one of them politely cut the portrait loose from its ornate frame and handed it to a grateful Emma.

The fire raged throughout the next day. Thousands of homeless poured out of the city in an endless stream, thieves looted, martial law was proclaimed, and buildings were blown up to make a fire break. For twenty-four hours Dwight and Emma had no idea whether their children had been trapped or saved, and Emma's hair started to turn gray. They hoped and prayed that Sankey had not been burned to death. Later they discovered that he had spent the night at lakeside with his little bundle of belongings. The next day, he took refuge in a boat on the lake.

By Wednesday the fire had burned out, but Chicago lay in ruins. Neighboring states provided some relief, much of it badly organized.

Everything he had labored for lay in shambles, so Dwight began to build again. Much of his ability resided in the area of solicitation: so he contacted all those who could possibly help in rebuilding. In Philadelphia George H. Stuart and John Wanamaker contributed generously. Then Dwight traveled to New York to meet with several wealthy prospects.

Writing to a would-be benefactor in New York on November 24, 1871, Dwight stated:

> *My dear Sir, you know something of the sad state of things in Chicago so far as the spiritual work is concerned. Fifty churches and missions are in ashes and the thousands of men, women, and children are without any Sabbath home. The temporal wants of the people are well supplied but there is no money to rebuild the churches and missions. The churches in the part of the city that was spared can do nothing. Their moneyed men are either bankrupt or as badly crippled as to prevent them from helping outside enterprises. My mission school and Free Church, on the North Side, went with the rest. . . . My plan is to raise $50,000 and put up a Tabernacle to accommodate seven or eight burnt out Missions. . . . Will you help us?*
>
> *Yours respectfully, D. L. Moody.*

The response to Dwight's efforts proved to be generous, but he could scarcely face the prospect of rebuilding. To be reduced almost to begging for funds disgusted him. Inwardly, he puzzled over his attitude. Didn't he believe in the work anymore? His heart certainly wasn't in pleading with others to give him money for these projects. He had done this so many times! No, his heart cried out for the filling of the Holy Spirit: that desire overwhelmed him and ruled over all others.

As he walked the streets of New York, he reviewed the situation. Farwell Hall and Illinois Street were in ashes, the ten or dozen committees had scattered like dying embers, nor could he face the exhaustion of reorganization. Had God burned him out that he should go all over the country, perhaps the world? But Dwight still said no. All the chains binding him to Chicago had snapped except one: his own will.

Dwight's inner turmoil continued unabated. He craved power! He began to march around New York streets at night, wrestling, panting for a Pentecost.

In broad daylight he walked down one of New York's busiest streets, Broadway or Fifth Avenue, he scarcely remembered which, while crowds jostled and pushed by and carriages and cabs jingled in the streets and newsboys shouted in his ears. The last chain snapped. Quietly, without a struggle, he surrendered.

Immediately an overpowering sense of God's presence flooded his soul. He felt as though Almighty God Himself had come to him. He needed to be alone in some private place. Quickly he hurried to the house of a nearby friend, disregarding an invitation to "come and have some food." Dwight told his friend softly, "I wish to be alone. Let me have a room where I can lock myself in."

His understanding host led him to a private room in the rear of the house, Dwight locked the door and sat on the sofa. The room seemed ablaze with God. He stretched out on the floor and lay bathing his soul in the Divine. Of this communion, this mountaintop experience he wrote later, "I can only say that God revealed Himself to me, and I had such an experience of His love that I had to ask Him to stay His hand."

The former turmoil vanished, conquered by an over-whelming sense of God's peace. Dwight's resolute will and determination suddenly came under new manage-ment as God remolded him and left him as gentle and tender as a baby.

No more would he choose his path. It was up to God to do that. He would lead, He would supply; Dwight need thirst no more. The dead dry days were gone. Thankfully, Dwight thought, *I was all the time tugging and carrying water. But now I have a river that carries me.*

Nearby a church clock chimed the quarter, the half, three quarters, the hour, and the hour again. Dwight lay still, hardly daring to move. Crazy Moody had become Moody, the man of God.

thirteen

New Vistas

Returning to Chicago within a short time, Dwight had three thousand dollars to start building a pine tabernacle. Incredibly, the building opened on Christmas Eve as a center of relief and evangelism. Dwight, his assistants, and Sankey slept in the drafty building. They placed boots over cracks to keep out some of the cold.

The whole area around the tabernacle still lay in a heap of rubble, but the tabernacle appeared as a beacon of light to many. Dwight had decided to "do the thing at hand," so he had dutifully returned to Chicago to rebuild the mission work. But he had determined not to be involved in any more committees!

A young man who visited the tabernacle for the New Year's Eve Watch Night Service on December 31, 1871, recorded his impression: "Consider the desolation all about. The midnight, the midwinter stillness, the yawning cellars and gaunt walls one had to pass walking southward for 45 minutes before reaching buildings and inhabited houses again. Ten below zero, a clear sky, a full moon overhead and absolute quiet." In the midst of the devastation, the young man came to the tabernacle, almost like a beacon to desperate souls. Filled almost to its 1,400-seat capacity, the tabernacle represented hope.

In January Dwight traveled to Brooklyn, New York, to hold a series of meetings in a new mission chapel. Afterward, a well-to-do layman, Morris K. Jessup, expressed his appreciation of Dwight: "The more I see of Moody the more I like him. I believe God is making him the instrument of a great work among the people." Jessup wanted Dwight to come to New York to live and work, but Dwight would have none of it.

Emma and Dwight continued on to Northfield following the New York meetings. On Sunday morning they attended the Trinitarian Congregational Church where the minister asked Dwight to speak.

A young girl, Eva Stebbins Callender, was impressed with the message. She usually became bored with the sermon, but "as soon as Mr. Moody began to talk I found to my surprise that I could understand him and I liked it. He told stories—and it was Sunday too—stories when he knew people could not help but laugh, and then it might be a story when the grown-ups would cry. He didn't preach, he only talked using the simplest language, sometimes with a loud voice as he denounced wrong doing." When Dwight pounded his fists on the pulpit cushion raising a cloud of dust and a tiny feather, everyone struggled to suppress their laughter!

That summer Dwight went by himself to the British Isles. He wanted as he put it "to study the English Christians" and to attend conventions and conferences, but primarily he desired to rest. Near Dublin a wealthy Plymouth Brother opened his mansion for a "Believers' Meeting" and here Dwight met "Butcher" Henry Varley again. All together, some twenty people met to spend a night in prayer. As Dwight left with Varley the next day, Varley let slip a remark that inspired Dwight: "The world has yet to see what God will do with a man fully consecrated to Him."

As Dwight pondered the phrase, he determined by the grace of God to be that man. Later, as he sat in Spurgeon's church, he realized for the first time that "it was not Spurgeon who was preaching: it was God. And if God could use Spurgeon, why should He not use me?"

Following this revelation, Dwight received an invitation to preach at Arundel Square near Pentonville Prison, in a lower-middle-class district of London. Visiting during the Sunday morning sermon, Dwight was irritated at the congregation's indifference. The people seemed to be lifeless and uninterested in anything the minister had to say. Dwight was tempted not to preach that night and wondered what message he could possible bring in the evening service that would have meaning for them. What could he say that would have an impact on the people's lives?

But that evening, as Dwight brought the message, the entire atmosphere seemed charged with electricity, and the congregation listened attentively and in quietness. In closing, he urged any who wanted "to have your lives changed by the power of God through faith in Jesus Christ as a personal Savior," wanted "to become Christians," to stand so he could pray for them. People stood all over the chapel.

Astonished, Dwight thought they had not understood and asked them to sit down. He stated again what becoming a Christian meant and then invited those who wished to do so to depart to an adjoining hall. He watched in amazement as scores of men, women, and older children made their way quietly to the connecting door. A school-room had been prepared as an inquiry room by setting out one or two dozen chairs. Many more chairs had to be added to seat the overflow crowd of people who expressed an interest in salvation.

Addressing the crowd, Dwight enlarged on repentance and faith, and again asked the people about becoming Christians. Once more, the whole room stood. In shock, Dwight told them to meet with their minister the following night.

The next morning, he left London, going to another part of England, but on Tuesday, he received a telegram urging him to come back to the London church. More people had come to the minister's meeting on Monday night than had been in the room on Sunday!

Returning to London, Dwight spoke at the Arundel Square Church each night for two weeks. Some fifty-three years later, a Baptist minister, James Sprunt, recalled that the results were staggering: "Four hundred were taken into the membership of that church, and by the grace of God I was one of that number."

Following this experience, Dwight returned to Chicago, but with several doors left ajar for him to come back to preach in England. He also wanted to return with a singer for any future meetings.

A wide-open door soon appeared in the form of a letter from William Pennefather in England. Mr. Penne-father, an outstanding evangelical Anglican, had heard Dwight preach and "was strongly impressed with the conviction that Mr. Moody was one for whom God had prepared a great work." In his letter to Dwight he told him "of the wide door open for evangelistic effort in London and elsewhere" and promised to help in whatever ways he could to guarantee the success of the venture.

Oddly, Dwight made no response to the letter. In fact, he had received invitations of a sort from two other individuals in England as well, Henry Bewley and Cuthbert Bainbridge, who had told him they would help with his expenses when he returned to England.

In Chicago, during the winter and spring of 1872-73, Dwight made it plain that he would not remain with the mission and tabernacle. He had helped rebuild and reestablish the work and felt no more desire to stay.

His heart now lay across the sea. Speaking at a conference held in Chicago's Second Presbyterian Church in the spring of 1873, Dwight said he wanted to dream great things for God—"To get back to Great Britain and win ten thousand souls!" When his elderly friend "Auntie" Cook asked him, "Are you going to preach to the miserable poor?" Dwight responded, "Yes, and to the miserable rich too!"

Although Dwight had not answered Pennefather's letter or responded to Bewley and Bainbridge, he thought an evangelistic tour was being organized for him, so he made plans to leave for England.

In the meantime, a letter came from a young chemist in the city of York, George Bennett, founder-secretary of the local YMCA. He and Dwight had met earlier, and he invited Dwight to speak at York. But Dwight failed to answer Bennett.

Even so, he continued to prepare for an evangelistic tour in England—one he thought was being organized for him. He tried to find a singer to accompany him, and unable to get Phillips or Bliss, finally settled on Sankey, who was considered an amateur compared to the others.

No more letters came from England except another one from George Bennett in York. Dwight responded to the letter indirectly through Morgan and Scott, religious publishers in London. Dwight's response was quite vague, stating he had "thought of coming" and since Bennett seemed earnest about having him preach, he might begin his tour at York.

With so little actual preparation, Dwight booked steamship passage for himself, Emma, their two children, and for Sankey and his wife on June 7, 1873. Farwell brought a gift of five hundred dollars; Dwight kept just fifty dollars, believing all his expenses would be paid!

The families managed to get to New York on the fifty dollars, but then Dwight had to wire Farwell to send the rest of the money.

At least while in New York, Dwight had notified Harry Moorhouse of his plans, so the small Englishman met the Moodys and Sankeys in Liverpool. He came on board ship and told them that Pennefather and Bain-bridge had both died recently and Henry Bewley must have forgotten his commitment to Dwight.

The families were stranded three thousand miles from home. Dwight looked at Sankey and observed, "God seems to have closed the doors. We'll not open any ourselves. If He opens the door we'll go in. If He don't we'll return to America."

As the Moodys and Sankeys talked and prayed about what to do, Dwight fired off a telegram to George Bennett in York. It read: "MOODY HERE ARE YOU READY FOR HIM?" Upon receiving the telegram, a shocked Mr. Bennett tried to decide what to do.

fourteen

Scotland Ablaze

O n June 18, 1873, while waiting in Liverpool for Bennett's reply, Dwight and his family were taken in by a shipowner interested in the YMCA, Richard Houghton. Harry Moorhouse hosted the Sankeys in Manchester. A reply came from Bennett on Friday morning asking Dwight to "PLEASE FIX DATE WHEN YOU CAN COME TO YORK. Dwight's response was immediate: "I WILL BE IN YORK TONIGHT TEN O'CLOCK STOP MAKE NO ARRANGEMENTS TILL I COME."

When Dwight descended from the train, he was met by a somewhat bewildered Bennett. That night over supper, the two men planned their strategy. Mr. Bennett apologized to Dwight for having the bed curtains covered up, but Dwight reassured him that, "I don't think the Lord Jesus had any curtains to His bed. What did for Him will do for me."

Sankey arrived Saturday afternoon and found Dwight in a jovial mood. "I say, Sankey," Dwight related, "here we are, a couple of white elephants! Bennett is away all over the city now, to see if he can get us a place. He's like a man who's got a white elephant and doesn't know what to do with it."

Bennett returned discouraged. Ministers were suspicious, saying things like: "Americans? Why do they want to come to York? What's the YMCA up to? Whoever heard of a mission in midsummer?" In spite of this, Bennett had been able to book the large and ugly Corn Exchange for Sunday afternoon. The Congregationalist deacons had grudgingly promised the morning pulpit at Salem Chapel because their new minister was away. Meanwhile, posters were being printed to advertise the meetings, and the news was being spread by word of mouth.

The Sunday morning message little affected the congregation made up of tradesmen and their families, a few footmen from the Deanery and Canons' houses, some soldiers from the barracks, a smattering of washerwomen, and railwaymen from back streets beyond the station. In the afternoon an undaunted Dwight and somewhat less confident Sankey walked with Bennett to the Corn Exchange. Dwight stopped at the YMCA and filled his arms with Bibles. He urged Sankey to get some too.

Mr. Bennett asked, "What do you want to do?"

With a twinkle in his eye, Dwight laughed and said, "Oh, I shall have your hair standing straight on your head before I have finished in York!"

Roughly eight hundred people waited in the Corn Exchange, which was not quite filled to capacity. Dwight ran around distributing Bibles here and there with a slip in each designating a Scripture number and reference.

He told them to read the text when he called our their number. The novel but effective Bible lecture that resulted on "God is Love" piqued their interest; the Yorkshire *Gazette* even reported on it.

The evening chapel services seemed lukewarm to

George Bennett, but the Spirit of God worked unseen in people's hearts. Many of them thought the songs Sankey led them in singing were strange—very different from the dirgelike hymns they thought proper for church services. Even though they were dignified and straitlaced, these same people later found themselves humming songs like "Hold the Fort" as they went about their daily chores.

When the charming Sankey sat at the little harmonium organ, his solos, with every word distinct, lifted hearers to worlds unknown and brought to their remembrance buried Christian teaching about God's love.

Dwight's preaching also shocked and intrigued. His hearers noted that he did not seek to score by denigrating the regular ministry. He let them know that he "preferred preaching in chapels and strengthening existing causes" to beginning any new work. He emphasized repeatedly that religion is a friendship and quoted, "'To as many as received Him, to them gave He power to become the sons of God.'" Then he would add: "Him, mark you! Not a dogma, not a creed, not a myth, but a Person." They noticed the blend of reverence and affection with which he would speak of "the Lord Jesus."

Dwight had also started a noon prayer meeting in a small room at the YMCA in Feasegate. The meeting turned out to be preparation for a great harvest.

On the second Wednesday, July 2, the Spirit's movement broke through the surface. Dwight spoke at the Wesleyan chapel on "Redeemed with the precious blood of Christ." Bennett witnessed that "the Holy Spirit's power was mightily manifested" and many people expressed great concern for their soul's salvation. Caught

up in the rapture of the moment, the elderly chapel superintendent could only weep for joy and astonishment.

Since that evening had been the last at the chapel, the
meeting moved to a new Baptist chapel on Priory Street.
The young minister, Frederick Brotherton Meyer, wondered what an evangelist would do that he could not do
himself. Meyer possessed flawless doctrine and deliber-
ate preaching, and he hesitated before opening his pulpit
to Dwight.

Dwight's retelling of the "Dying Teacher" whom
he accompanied back in Chicago failed to move the
Reverend F. B. Meyer. But when Meyer casually asked
the woman who taught the senior girls' class her opinion,
she blurted out: "Oh, I told that story again and I believe
every one of my girls has given her heart to God!"

Her response shook Meyer, and he began to watch
intently night after night as the moderate-sized chapel,
vestries, lobbies, and even the pulpit stairs were crowded with people. Each night he also watched reverently as
the people crowded his minister's parlor, seeking the
knowledge of salvation.

As an old man, F. B. Meyer remembered Moody's visit:
"For me it was the birthday of new conceptions of ministry, new methods of work, new inspirations and hopes."
After going into the ministry, Meyer admitted his lack of
spiritual understanding: "I didn't know anything about
conversion, or about the gathering of sinners around
Christ. I owe everything in my life to that parlor room
where for the first time I found people brokenhearted
about sin. I learned the psychology of the soul. I learned
how to point men to God."

The revival didn't spread to other areas, so both Dwight and Sankey sent for their families to join them. They were quite homesick. Dwight implored Farwell to send full details of the YMCA and mission in Chicago, and Sankey complained that the sun near the arctic circle kept him from sleeping.

After a brief foray to Sunderland for a "campaign," as Dwight began to call his meetings, the evangelists were invited to Newcastle-upon-Tyne, twelve miles northwest of Sunderland. Despite mild opposition to the Americans, Dwight determined when he arrived on August 25, "to stick there until prejudice died."

By the end of September, a distinguished Scottish Presbyterian minister, John Cairns, who also held a part-time professorship in Edinburgh, passed through Newcastle. He wrote his sister about the meeting: "There was a great crowd at Mr. Leitch's church; and the chief peculiarity was the singing by a Mr. Sankey with harmonium accompaniment under the direction of a Mr. Moody, an American gentleman who has been laboring in Newcastle for five weeks. The singing was impressive, the congregation striking in at the choruses with thrilling effect." Cairns went on to say that everyone in the vicinity spoke warmly of the meetings and of their results.

Suddenly Dwight and Sankey had jumped from the obscurity of York to being the talk of the greatest city in northern England.

The Newcastle campaign had started among the well-churched middle classes and slowly spread upward and downward. Rich merchants, shipbuilders, and coal-mine owners began to attend after the Newcastle *Chronicle* praised the "wonderful religious phenomenon."

The article especially acclaimed the meetings' "lack of sectarianism, the single-mindedness of Moody," and the fact that no offerings were taken.

One class that Dwight longed to reach, but that had not yet attended were the "Geordies," the people of the slums. They had to work long hours underground, barely existed on scanty diets, and breathed coal dust day and night.

Dwight created an opportunity to reach this class when a baby cried at one of his meetings. Instead of censoring the mother and demanding the baby be taken out, he decided then and there to hold "Mother's Meetings," that no one could attend without a baby. The lower-class women flocked to these meetings, and Dwight was gratified that he could now reach out to these poorer classes.

Increasing attendance also brought a demand for copies of the hymns which Sankey sang, especially of "Jesus of Nazareth Passeth By." Sankey had the only copies and wrote to the English publishers of Philip Phillips' collection, offering his own selection without charge if they would print it as a supplement. The publisher refused, and Dwight promised another publisher, Richard Cope Morgan of Morgan and Scott, to guarantee an edition of a sixteen-page pamphlet of Sankey's selection.

On September 16, *Sacred Songs and Solos* appeared in its first short form at sixpence a copy, or a penny for words only, to be used in alliance with Phillips' book, which was also on sale.

Moody and Sankey had affected the churches in England's northeast corner, although many ministers still looked with disdain on unaccredited lay preachers from America—or anywhere else.

As Dwight planned where to go next and tentatively considered a nine-day opportunity in Darlington and some other small towns, a Scottish minister, the Reverend John Kelman, approached him after the evening meeting.

"Come to Edinburgh. I and my friends of the Free and Established Churches will form a committee. We will prepare the ground, and I believe that every presbytery will support you. Win Edinburgh, and you will win Scotland. Scotland needs you!"

Speechless, Dwight hardly knew to respond. Could it be that Edinburgh, the Athens of the North, would really receive a man who had little formal education and still lapsed into poor grammar in unguarded moments? Then he thought about the able Presbyterian theologians, dry scholars of intense earnestness, grave, discriminating, rigid, who would be on the platform. His rapid torrent of anecdote and informal Bible teaching might shock or irritate.

And what about Sankey? Most Scotsmen considered the singing of anything other than metrical versions of the Psalms to be offensive. Lamely, Dwight suggested accepting a prior invitation to Dundee, but Kelman was emphatic. "Come to Edinburgh first. Then you will reach the nation."

Unable to give an immediate answer, Dwight needed time to think, to pray about his decision. This was so momentous an opportunity—the first one to work in a capital city prepared by a representative committee.

121

Edinburgh's leading men of religion, Kelman assured him, would stand behind him. Dwight thought, *That is only an opinion!*

If he accepted the offer, it would be at the risk of being made Britain's laughingstock. Never would he be able to show his face again in the British Isles.

The Moody and Sankey families arrived in Edinburgh at Waverley Station on November 22, 1873, on a stormy Saturday night. The Sankeys had been invited to stay with Horatius Bonar, the veteran hymn writer; the Moodys were to be guests of William Blaikie, a friend of David Livingstone.

The first meeting began the next evening on Princes Street. While the committee tried to estimate the attendance, Sankey could see the city's largest hall "densely packed to its utmost corners; even the lobbies, stairs, and entrance were crowded with people, while more than two thousand were turned away." All these people made Sankey nervous. He had heard the complaints about his "human" hymns and even more against his "kist o' whustles" as the Scots called the little harmonium organ that accompanied him.

The chairman's announcement at the outset that Mr. Moody, due to a sore throat, would not attend that evening brought gasps of disappointment.

Sankey stood up and invited the congregation to sing with him a familiar tune, the "Old Hundredth." When he sang "Jesus of Nazareth Passeth By," an intense silence pervaded the huge audience. Sankey felt reassured about the merit of "human" hymns to work in people's hearts. Following the address given by James Hood Wilson of the Barclay Free Church, Sankey concluded with "Hold the Fort," and to his delight, the congregation joined wholeheartedly in the chorus.

After spending the day spraying his throat with medicine, Dwight rejoined Sankey the following night in Barclay Church. Dwight had his work cut out for him in the formidable Scottish religious climate.

Extreme Calvinism had long held sway in the majority of churches. In fact, Old Testament Law had been deemed superior to "the royal law of love," the "joy of the Lord" had been defeated by rules and regulations, and most people believed it blasphemy to claim the certainty of going to heaven. They would say that though Christ had died for all, none knew whether he or she was predestined to salvation.

Because of this extreme Calvinism, many of the lower classes never attended church at all; on the other hand, the educated classes were racked by doubt and unbelief which had led to much division and suspicion among the churches of Scotland.

In spite of this unfavorable religious atmosphere, an elderly saint, R. S. Candlish, shortly before his death the previous fall, had prophesied a great blessing which should not be despised—though it came strangely.

Night after night the people came. A participant, Hood Wilson, noted: "The church was crowded in every part and every spot of standing ground occupied. A number have come to peace in believing—some of them the most unlikely."

The Scots took to Dwight immediately and even excused and enjoyed his profuse diction which stopped

neither for colons nor commas. They tolerated his
Yankee accent and forgave him for sometimes deliber-
ately making them laugh in church. His audiences found
themselves surprised by joy.

Growing more confident through his open acceptance,
Dwight's assertiveness in the power of Christ to save
continued to increase. There were no sudden breaks as
there had been during services at York, no groping for
words. A steady brightening like some spring sun-
rise dispelling the chill November gray filled people's
hearts as men and women grasped the astonishing fact
that God loves sinners; they had believed He loved only
saints.

The audience listened enthralled as Dwight shared
with them his convictions. One night he told them about
a young man who thought himself too great a sinner to
be saved. Dwight's response: "Why, they are the very
men Christ came after! 'This man receiveth sinners, and
eateth with them.' The only charge they could bring
against Christ down here was that He was receiving bad
men. They are the very kind of men He is willing to
receive. All you have got to do is to prove that you are a
sinner and I will prove that you have got a Savior." Then
he would tell his audience an anecdote about someone
he knew who came to know Christ.

His hearers scarcely believed their ears. It sounded
so simple. Scottish preaching for many years had emphasized cold, dry doctrine and told its adherents that they
were the subject of God's wrath. The only way to obtain
forgiveness was by believing in a complex theological
puzzle.

For these strangers to appear suddenly and begin expounding a theology that God didn't "hate" them was a shock. Time was required for these new ideas to sink in. Moody and Sankey stressed God's goodness and forgiveness, a simple but welcome new idea.

When Dwight kept his messages down to less than an hour in length and interspersed them with silent prayer or a song from Sankey, the Scots thought the American duo even more novel. They expected a sermon to last at least an hour and a half.

Another novel aspect to the Scots was that Dwight made no attempt to play on their emotions through sensation or excitement; he also provoked "no articulate wailings, no prostrations, no sudden outbursts of rapture" found in other revivals, according to one observer.

Nevertheless, Dwight preached for decision. People had to choose Christ as their Savior. He would not acquiesce to suit Calvinistic hesitancy which feared lest appeal for a definite step of faith overrode predestination—a word Dwight could barely pronounce!

He placed his emphasis "upon the doctrine that Christianity is not mere feeling, but a surrender of the whole nature to a personal, living Christ," said Mr. Blaikie, a campaign associate. Inquiry, room sessions after each meeting played a pivotal part in a person's decision for Christ.

Some people expressed suspicions about the inquiry, thinking it might be an emotional "forcing house," or a complete surrender to an unbalanced doctrine of free will. Some even feared that it was a dark imitation of the Roman Catholic confessional. These fears quieted as ministers had personal contact with the work and with the inquirers themselves.

The methods advocated in dealing with the inquirers were new, too. Dwight urged the "personal workers," as he called them, patience and "thorough dealing with each case, no hurrying from one to another. Wait patiently and ply them with God's word, and think, oh! think, what it is to win a soul for Christ, and don't grudge the time spent on one person."

By the middle of December, several weeks after the meetings began, Edinburgh had been stirred to its depths. The meetings were on everyone's mind. Many had been strengthened and helped, and unity began to appear in Scottish churches and even among the clergy.

An Edinburgh University professor, Professor Charteris, said that "if anyone had said that the sectarian divisions which are so visible not only in ecclesiastical concerns but in social life and in private friendships would disappear in the presence of two evangelists who came among us with no such ecclesiastical credentials, the idea would have seemed absolutely absurd." The results in unity turned out to be so far-reaching that decades later, the Scots still rejoiced at what God had accomplished through Dwight L. Moody and Ira Sankey.

God used these two Americans to reform stiff, conservative Edinburgh in other ways as well. The campaign committee had started a prayer meeting before the onset of the larger gatherings. After sitting through a number of long, scriptural, doctrinal, somewhat controversial, and vague prayers, Dwight banged his fist on the table. Everyone sat bolt upright as he stated somewhat impatiently: "I tell you, friends, some people's prayers need to be cut at both ends and set fire to in the middle!" His point made, the prayers shortened considerably. But the Scots could receive the brief reprimand more from Dwight than from one of their own.

Sankey, too, and his little harmonium organ became popular. The Scots' distrust of "human" hymns had almost completely disappeared. Sankey sang some of Horatius Bonar's hymns in the nightly meetings, and Bonar began to achieve acceptance along with Sankey.

By January 1874, news of the revival in Edinburgh had spread all over Scotland. The leading Edinburgh ministers and laymen sent out an "Appeal for Prayer" to every minister of every denomination in Scotland. The ministers also collected a special fund to provide a weekly copy of "The Christian" to send to each minister throughout the British Isles. The publication carried special reports about the meetings.

One of the ministers in the small village of Inverkip found himself caught up in the revival though he was miles away. His preaching and praying took on new life. He called for a Sunday night "testimony meeting." The people didn't even know what it was, but they ended up touched and revived as well as their minister.

Sudden fame had come to thirty-eight-year-old Dwight and his thirty-five-year-old song leader. Dwight knew he was merely the recipient of a higher power and remained humble, but Sankey probably enjoyed the new status. He stood more erect and had a new spring in his step.

What else did God have for this amazing evangelistic

duo? Were there new worlds to conquer? The next summons they received came from Glasgow—another bastion of Scottish conservatism and strict Calvinism. They were ready.

fifteen

*F*ollowing a few weeks in Dundee, Dwight and Sankey and their families arrived in Glasgow. The people there had made full preparations for the campaign: they had readied massed choirs, covered the meetings with prayer in large prayer meetings, and distributed tickets for people to attend the nightly meetings to avoid unsafe overcrowding.

Dwight and his family stayed with Andrew Bonar, who was a well-known Bible teacher. He came into Dwight's life at just the right time. Dwight had been giving out to the people night after night and was in danger of spiritual drought. Ecstatic over Bonar's biblical wisdom and insight, Dwight would call to a friend to "come and join us! We are having a dig in the Rock!" He remarked later that Bonar was one of the two men in Britain who helped him most in understanding the depths of the Bible.

The campaign opened at nine on Sunday morning, February 8, in the City Hall with three thousand Sunday school teachers. After Andrew Bonar's opening prayer, Sankey began to sing "I Am So Glad That Jesus Loves Me," a tune written by Phillip Bliss. Although unknown to most of the audience, the song ministered to people's hearts. David Russell, one of the teachers present, told how Sankey enraptured him: "I had never heard such magnificent singing. The great consecrated voice, the glad face of the singer, and the almost childish simplicity of the words overcame me, and I found tears streaming down my face. I felt ashamed lest anyone should see my weakness, but before long I noticed tears on other faces."

Also impressive to Mr. Russell was the way Dwight held his Bible in his right hand, indicative of his hold on it and its hold on him. The American accent and what at first appeared to be a lack of reverence and dignity caused Mr. Russell to think he wouldn't like Dwight. However, after Dwight told his first story, he endeared himself to his audience.

So powerful was the meeting that morning that Dwight and Sankey were carried along on a revival tide. Week after week through the cheerless, cold winter and on into spring, the meetings continued in churches, the City Hall, and last of all, in the Kibble Palace, an enormous glass exhibition building generally called the Crystal Palace. People came by every means possible: on foot, by horse-tram, by train, in carriages, and in cabs. They came from every walk of life to attend the meetings: from shipyards, mills, tenements, and the surrounding middle-class homes.

Dwight's amazing energy also impressed people. Dutifully, Sankey managed to keep up with him. A newspaper commented on their daily schedule: "The mind experiences a sense of fatigue in detailing their efforts. On Weekdays, the huge hourly prayer meeting is held at noon; one to two o'clock, they converse with individuals; four to five o'clock, they have a Bible lecture, attended by some twelve or fifteen hundred; seven to eight-thirty, the evangelistic meeting takes place with the inquiry meeting afterward; and nine to ten o'clock, the young men hold a meeting."

A Scottish friend of Dwight's observed that, "he had strength and used it unsparingly, but people seemed to think it had no limit." He reserved one day a week for relaxing, usually on Saturday.

Having already put in a full day, Dwight especially relished the young men's meetings at day's end. But the one on Tuesday, February 24, became known across Scotland as the "Hundred-and One Night." While Dwight still preached at City Hall, the Young Men's Meeting got underway in Ewing Place Church. It was packed from floor to ceiling. Five Edinburgh students led by Henry Drummond gave brief, rousing appeals. Hood Wilson then asked, "Why not tonight?" Dwight came in about this time, and as Wilson finished, he said quietly, "All those who are sure they are Christians, stand up.

"Sit down again, please! The three pews in front here, I want them cleared. Anyone who wants to take Christ as their Savior, you all come forward now, so we can pray for you. Let us bow our heads as they come."

People began to come forward in utter quietness. A stream of people flowed from every part of the building. Dwight lifted his eyes, prayed aloud, and to one of the Edinburgh students, James Stalker, "the sense of Divine power became overwhelming, and I remember quite well turning round on the platform and hiding my face in my hands, unable to look on the scene any more." As the front seats filled, Dwight cleared the next rows, and the next.

An usher counted one hundred and one inquirers who came forward, and Christian counselors stayed until midnight, praying and ministering to the seekers. Near the end, a young man said he had been seeking Christ a long time but was leaving without finding relief. Just then Dwight came over and "took me kindly by the hand. He looked at me—I might say he put his two eyes right through mine—and asked me if I would take Christ now. I could not speak, but my heart said 'Yes.' "

In the hotel afterward, the five Edinburgh student leaders talked far into the night about the remarkable scene they had just witnessed. They were able to keep in touch with many of the young men who came forward that night and were pleased that most remained active Christians. Many of them continued to help in the Moody campaign until it moved on.

"For the last three months I have had to refuse money all the time!" wrote Dwight to his Chicago friend Whittle on March 7, 1874. "At Edinburgh they wanted to raise me two or three thousand pounds but I would not let them. I told them I would not take it."

Not only did Dwight refuse personal money, but he also turned down collections for campaign funds. Letters had appeared in the papers asserting the whole campaign to be a glorious hoax organized for gain by Barnum, the American showman. As Dwight explained to Farwell, "Of course I have a good many enemies over here who say I am a speculating Yankee." He would tell the campaign committee to raise funds privately, and very occasionally he accepted personal gifts "to myself for my own use," beyond hospitality and expenses.

But Dwight stayed adamant about preaching "for filthy lucre." He realized the temptations involved with money, and the Scottish people despite their renown for thrift, wanted to shower him with finances. Much of what he received, he sent on to help another evangelistic team in America, Whittle and Bliss. The money would help them abandon their businesses and devote full time to ministry. Dwight told them, "If you have not got faith enough launch out on the strength of my faith." He stressed, "Has not our God got as much money as the Watch Company & all he wants of us is to trust Him?" Of course, Dwight's own faith seemed as expansive as his personality.

Wealthy individuals such as chemical manufacturer Campbell White were lavish in extending money to Dwight, and many people thought he was amassing a small fortune. He reached the wealthier classes, but always his heart was stirred over the poor. Many of them would not attend the meetings, so Dwight urged wealthy men to reach out to the poor after the campaign was over.

To Dwight's delight, the United Evangelistic Committee reformed to become the Glasgow Evangelistic Association and began a long career in evangelism and philanthropy, spawning agencies such as Poor Children's Day Refuges, Temperance Work, Fresh Air Fortnights, the Cripple Girls' League, and the Glasgow Christian Institute. On Sunday mornings on Glasgow

Green, young men brought in the homeless and derelicts for a free breakfast.

Sir George Adam Smith, who differed theologically from Dwight, offered a positive testimony following the Moody campaign: "We have forgotten how often Mr. Moody enforced the civic duties of our faith. Yet read again his addresses and articles of the time, and you will believe that in the seventies there was no preacher more practical or civic amongst us."

Of course there were bound to be detractors, and Dwight's daily mail brought in hundreds of letters, many that were critical. They were everywhere! His host, Hood Wilson, said the library had become "a perfect sea of letters, which were not only an inch deep on the large round table in the middle of the room, but covered chairs and shelves in every corner."

One of the strongest criticisms came in the form of a pamphlet circulated by an influential Highland preacher, John Kennedy. In the pamphlet, entitled "Hyper-evangelism: 'Another Gospel' Though a Mighty Power," Kennedy charged that, "the present movement ignores the sovereignty and power of God," that the emphasis on faith hindered the work of the Holy Spirit and denied "the utter spiritual impotence of souls 'dead in trespasses and sins.' "

Kennedy blasted the inquiry room, the singing of "human" hymns, the use of organ music ("unscriptural, and therefore all who have subscribed the Confession of Faith are under solemn vow against it"), and alleged that prayer meetings had been turned into "factories of sensation."

Such attacks from rigid High Calvinism could be expected. Dwight said he could have pointed out more faults in his work himself! But he sensed criticism must be coming from other sources as well to account for the subtly poisoned atmosphere that was beginning to surround the campaign.

While Dwight pondered how to squelch the vicious attack from someone the simple Highlanders revered, he received a letter from a Chicago acquaintance. John Mackay, a lawyer and recent Scottish emigrant, had circulated a scathing letter denigrating Dwight. He told how "Mr. Moody came to Chicago a poor lad. . .called at the office of a pious and wealthy city merchant and begged him for a place in his office. Mr. Moody worked himself into the confidence of the house." The letter went on to say that Dwight got hold of some "secrets" of his employer and passed them on to an opponent in court, causing him to win a pending lawsuit.

The letter stated that, "Moody stoutly denied the charge . . .Undeniable proof. . .he confessed and was discharged . . . . Soon afterwards publicly declared his determination to devote himself wholly to the Lord's work. . ."

Possessed of much common sense, Dwight met this attack head-on. He wrote Farwell on May 7, relating the letter's charges against him. He then asked Farwell to have Mr. Henderson, a nephew of Dwight's earlier employer, write a letter "expressing confidence in me." Dwight asked Henderson's forgiveness for any unseemly attitude while employed for his uncle, giving his youth as an excuse. Dwight added, "No one knows me here and if my friends in Chicago do not stand by me, who will? For everyone in this country who is opposed to my preaching and revivals are doing all they can to break me down. Please write me at once."

Soon afterward, Farwell secured the signatures of thirty-five Chicago ministers to an endorsement of Moody's Christian character, and he cabled the document to Edinburgh. Henderson wrote, "For fifteen years since Mr. Moody left us I have watched him, assisted him and believed in him."

Farwell demanded a retraction, but the Scottish immigrant refused to do so. Then Farwell threatened him with the law, but Dwight would not pursue litigation.

In the final days of the Glasgow campaign, even the invective of Kennedy could not destroy what God had accomplished. On the last Sunday in May, the Great Western Road leading to the campaign site had been black for over three hours with an endless stream of humanity.

That day Dwight preached in the Botanical Gardens from the box of a carriage to a crowd estimated at twenty or thirty thousand.

Afterward, he readied himself to return to English soil.

sixteen

Revival fires continued to burn in Scotland long after the Moody/Sankey campaign. Andrew Murray of South Africa, returning to Scotland a few years later, noticed "very distinctly the influence of Mr. Moody's work. There is much more readiness to talk out and much more warmth. . . . The whole religious tone of Scotland has been lifted up and brightened most remarkably."

Prior to leaving Scotland, and after a brief leisurely trip to Loch Ness and the Caledonian Canal, Dwight preached a few more times near Campbelltown where he and his family stayed with Peter and Jane Mackinnon.

The Mackinnons and Moodys found great compatibility. Dwight remarked that Peter, a partner with the British India Line, became like a father to him more so than "any man that has crossed my path."

Treasuring Dwight's famous anecdotes, Jane made note of several when he stayed with them. Returning from a meeting on a windy night, he remarked, "The gas made such a noise, it roared and I had to roar, and it was a battle between us, but I think I won!"; how the custodian kept opening a door which Dwight shut because a draught interfered with the inquiry work, so he locked it and put the key in his pocket; how he would inspect a church for ventilation before speaking and had all his wits about him even for the smallest details. Jane noticed his decisiveness: "'You just listen to me, and do what I tell you,' he would urge his helpers." She also realized his flexibility in the services: "He said he never knew, even a few minutes before, what he was going to do. I suppose he asks guidance at every step, and is sure he gets it."

Jane enjoyed both Moodys and thought them good company. She especially liked Dwight's combination of playfulness and seriousness. "It was delightful having him at leisure; he is so simple, so unaffected and lovable; he plays so heartily with the children, and makes fun with those who can receive it. He is brimful of humor." He also played croquet and helped the children catch crabs on the beach.

Emma, too, won a place in Jane Mackinnon's heart. She saw at once how valuable Emma was to Dwight: "The more I saw of her, the more convinced I was that a great deal of his usefulness was owing to her, not only in the work she did for him, relieving him of all correspondence, but also from her character." Jane became aware of Emma's independence of thought, her humility, and especially the calmness with which she met Dwight's impulsiveness.

When telegrams arrived urging Dwight to "squeeze in a visit" to yet another place, and he asked her, "Which way should I go? I really don't know what to do," Emma would not sway him. She would say, "It's up to you; you decide, tell me, and I'll write."

But Emma always had the last word. Just after their twelfth wedding anniversary (while at the Mackinnons), Emma wrote her mother in Chicago telling her, "Mr. Moody is nicer and kinder every day. He is a gem of a husband. I ought to be very happy."

The Moodys rejoined Sankey in Belfast, Ireland, where the crowds were similar to those of Edinburgh and Glasgow; then they traveled to Dublin, although Dwight had been warned against going there because of its Roman Catholic majority. As usual, Dwight called the warning foolishness and proceeded full-speed ahead.

For the first time, Dwight and Sankey had the full support of Anglicans, including several bishops of the recently disestablished Church of Ireland. But Dwight stunned the Irish by refusing to attack Roman Catholics. His refusal opened the door for everyone of whatever religious persuasion to attend the meetings.

The campaign became the center of conversation, and even music halls were not exempt from having fun over the evangelists' names. At one music hall, a comic turned to another and said: "I am rather Moody tonight. How do you feel?"

"Sankeymonious!"

The gallery hissed. Someone started singing "Hold the Fort," and the whole audience began to join in while the comedians fled the stage.

Even the leading newspapers commented on the campaign, and the Dublin *Times* correspondent noted favorably that the campaign was "the most remarkable ever witnessed in Ireland; it had a character essentially different and seemed to possess elements of vitality wanting in others." In particular the correspondent was impressed with "the reverence and devotion of the services," and "not only the absence of any effort at self-display but rather a sensitive avoidance of it."

As the campaign came to a close, ministers and laity from every part of Ireland joined together in a great "Christian Convention for Ireland." The meeting was held at the Exhibition Palace with thousands in attendance. The submerging of bitter sectarian feelings caused wonderment to many but became almost a trademark of Dwight's wherever he went. His touch could be felt in the committee's arrangement that clergymen from a distance were lodged with clerical families of denominations other than their own.

By November 1874, the Moody and Sankey families crossed the Irish Sea to Liverpool and on to Manchester, England. Harry Moorhouse waited to greet them. He welcomed them with open arms, rejoicing that "success has not made Dwight proud. He uses his ten talents, I use my one, and we both together praise the Lord for using us at all."

Dwight held campaigns in Manchester, Sheffield, and Birmingham in quick succession with good results in each place. A Church of England newspaper, the *Record,* reported, "There is a degree of religious feeling in the town which has not been equalled for years."

Reaching Birmingham later in January, Dwight preached to large crowds at Bingley Hall. The effect of the campaign climaxed in some doggerel verse sold on the street corners:

> *Oh, the town's upside down, everybody seems mad,*
> *When they come to their senses we all shall feel glad,*
> *For the rich and the poor, and the good and the bad,*
> *Are gone mad over Moody and Sankey.*

Thrilled over such an unusual opportunity, an Anglican clergyman wrote of the Birmingham campaign, "Such a chance of guiding souls comes only once in a lifetime."

One puzzled minister, Dr. Dale of Carr's Lane Congregational Church in Birmingham, had been expecting a revival for a few years. But he expressed bewilderment when it came through two American strangers.

Watching the attentive faces of the huge crowd at Bingley Hall, he saw "all sorts, young and old, rich and poor, keen tradesmen, manufacturers and merchants and young ladies who had just left school, rough boys who knew more about dogs and pigeons than about books, and cultivated women. . . . I could not understand it."

Dr. Dale told Dwight, "The work is most plainly of God, for I can see no relation between yourself and what you have done." Dwight chuckled in his inimitable way and told him, "I should be very sorry if it were otherwise."

Many others expressed wonder, too, that an American should be the one God used in this revival, although the church had been diligent to pray for some time before Moody arrived.

Probably much of Dwight's success lay in his simple

preaching. As Dr. Dale noted, "He talks in a perfectly unconstrained and straightforward way, just as he would talk to half a dozen old friends at his fireside."

The English preachers, on the other hand, were given to an ornate style of preaching. Spurgeon, for example, piled metaphor upon metaphor, but Dwight simply chatted about what he saw in the Bible.

He made the Bible come alive in everyday language. Daniel in the lions' den looks at his watch to see if it is time to pray. Scoffers before the Flood "talk it over in the corner grocery store: 'Not much sign of old Noah's rainstorm yet!' "

Blind Bartimaeus, suddenly able to see, rushes into Jericho "and he says, 'I will go and see my wife and tell her about it'—a young convert always wants to talk to his friends about salvation—Away he goes down the street 'n' he meets a man who passes him 'n' goes on a few yards 'n' then turns round 'n' says, 'Bartimaeus, is that you?' 'Yes.' 'Well, I thought it was, but I couldn't believe my eyes! How've you gotten your sight?' 'Oh, I just met Jesus of Nazareth outside the city and asked Him to have mercy on me.' 'Jesus of Nazareth! What! Is He in this part of the country?' 'Sure. Right here in Jericho.' 'I should like to see him!' and away he runs down the street."

Or it was Zaccheus (or "Zakkus" as Dwight would say) sitting in the sycamore tree. So the sermon would shift from one scene to another of Christ meeting people in their need.

Somehow when Dwight preached, he would fade from his hearers' consciousness. Someone remarked about this ability: "Throughout his address you entirely forgot the man, so full was he of his message and so held were you by his earnestness, intensity, and forceful appeal. He had many illustrations drawn from his personal experiences, but never did self appear prominent. He was completely absorbed in the message and in getting it over to the mind, heart, and conscience of those listening."

In Liverpool at a men's meeting, several rationalistic thinkers were present who did not acknowledge Christ's death on the cross. But as Dwight prayed in the speakers' room before the service, Reverend F. B. Meyer found himself awed by Dwight's overpowering "burden of heart."

After Dwight preached that night, large numbers stayed for the after-meeting. Dwight came down from the platform, got up on a chair, "and launched out in a wonderful discourse. His invectives against sin, and his lashings of the conscience, were awful. He seemed to be wrestling with an unseen power. Beneath those burning words men's faces grew pale under a conviction of the broken law of God. Then he began with the wooings of the Gospel, in a strain of tender and heartbreaking entreaty; by the time he finished, the whole audience seemed completely broken. One man arose and said, 'Mr. Moody, I want to be a Christian.' It seemed but a moment when forty or fifty men were on their feet."

The England Dwight had come to had been primed on Christian doctrine, and most people knew something about Christ and about the Bible. However, Christianity had gained respectability in the Victorian age to the point where sins of the flesh had been concealed behind a veneer of the spirit. Dwight was able to pierce through the hypocritic veil many wore.

More importantly, real Christianity had been distorted by an ineffective gospel that preached a good person would go to heaven, a wicked one to hell. Little was known or taught of God's grace. Against this warped teaching, Dwight proclaimed eternal life as the gift of God to the undeserving. He did not deny eternal punishment for those who refused this gift, but he would say, "I believe the magnet that goes down to the bottom of the pit is the love of Jesus."

A popular example Dwight used to illustrate the difference between law and grace was the story of the Prodigal Son. "When the prodigal came home, grace met him and embraced him. Law said, Stone him! —grace said, Embrace him! Law said, Smite him!—grace said, Kiss him! Law went after him and bound him. Grace said, Loose him and let him go! Law tells me how crooked I am; grace comes and makes me straight."

Dwight's message emphasized that God wanted men more than they wanted Him. He proclaimed that salvation was not a grudged reward for a consistent climb into goodness but the new birth of a repentant sinner into the life of Christ. "Instant salvation," he called it over and over. His preaching, said Dr. Dale "was in a manner that produced the sort of effect produced by Luther, and provoked similar criticism. He exulted in the free grace of God. His joy was contagious. Men leaped out of darkness into light, and lived a Christian life afterwards."

Not since the days of Wesley and Whitefield had people from so many social classes found joy in Christ.

Some of the very poor people had been helped by General William Booth and the Salvation Army, but at last many of the middle and upper classes were also discovering salvation in Christ.

Dwight had preached in the provinces, but he knew that for the movement to become national, he must win London. The London committee made up of the clergy, members of Parliament, and high-ranking officers had done much preparation work for the Moody campaign. They had inundated London with posters and notices of all kinds and had organized teams to visit the entire city. They had also secured the Agricultural Hall in Islington for at least a ten-week stretch. The home of the annual prize cattle show in north London's principal middle class area, the Agricultural Hall had been freshly refurbished and fifteen thousand chairs installed.

On opening night the hall was in readiness with seats on the left for participants and distinguished guests, a railed pulpit area in the middle, and on the right seating room for a two-hundred member choir. Red banners hung all around the hall proclaiming such texts as: "Repent ye and believe the gospel," "The gift of God is eternal life," and "Ye must be born again."

When Dwight and Sankey stepped onto the platform at seven-thirty, and Dwight told the audience: "Let us rise and sing to the praise of God, Let us praise Him for what He is going to do in London," a wave of expectancy swept over the tremendous crowd.

The London *Daily Telegraph* correspondent, who perhaps couldn't see Dwight too clearly, described him as tall, if stout, with a "not unintellectual cast of countenance." He said he felt relief to discover that Dwight was "altogether as unlike the conventional 'ranter' as it is possible to conceive," and with some British snobbery assured readers that Moody had little American about him except "a strange Western twang." Sankey, he said, could "be mistaken for an Englishman anywhere."

The newspaper article spoke quite favorably of Dwight and the campaign, generally calling Dwight's stories "good American stories picked up in Chicago." The reporter commended the campaign's tone that pointed the way for men and women to become better, and for them to have "a better hope in this world and the next."

Dwight knew from the outset of the campaign, however, there would be opposition. He warned his committee: "We must expect opposition. If you think a great work is to be done here without opposition you will be greatly mistaken. There will be many bitter things said, and many lies started, and as someone has said, a lie will get half round the world before the truth gets its boots on!"

He spoke accurately; before long, articles in the *Morning Post* called his teaching "wild, baseless, and uncertain. Moody and Sankey will be a puff in the wind." In the *Morning Advertiser,* people read, "There must have been thousands in that crowd of uplifted faces who looked with horror and shame on the illiterate preacher making little better than a travesty of all they held sacred." The article played on the word "vulgar," calling Moody's accent vulgar and stating he was "a ranter of the most vulgar type."

There were other more penetrating criticisms that

could not be easily dismissed: "Where the corpulent old expounder is known he is regarded as a selfish, sensual, hypocritical variegator of facts." And poor Sankey was accused of starting his career as a black "minstrel" until he found that evangelism paid better. The article also stressed all the money the two evangelists were making. They would return to America and "gaze upon their cosy homesteads purchased with good English gold" and claim that they had "spoiled the Egyptians."

Actually, Dwight and Sankey had refused to touch the considerable money from *Sacred Songs and Solos* and had worked out an arrangement with Hugh Matheson to give the royalties to worthy charities.

Despite libel and criticism, attendance at the Agricultural Hall rose to an estimated twenty thousand. More space was made for an overflow crowd. Even the Lord Chancellor of Disraeli's new Conservative Government, Mr. Cairns, attended the meetings frequently. And former Prime Minister Gladstone talked privately with Dwight, also sitting on the platform once or twice. Dwight had remarked that "Gladstone is a converted man and a true and humble Christian."

Gladstone had exclaimed to a friend how thankful he was that "I have lived to see the day when He should bless His church on earth by the gift of a man able to preach the Gospel of Christ as we have just heard it preached!"

Complimenting Dwight on his powerful voice, Gladstone said, "I wish I had your chest, Mr. Moody!"

Dwight came back with: "And I wish I had your head on top of it!"

Although the crowds overflowed night after night at Agricultural Hall, Lord Shaftesbury, a recent ally of Dwight's, thought he should move to the Queen's Opera House where he could reach the upper classes of people. Dwight expressed reluctance, but finally acquiesced to at least have afternoon Bible readings in the Opera House.

The wonderful response to the afternoon Bible readings caused Dwight to turn over the Agricultural Hall meetings to an associate nine days early and begin evening meetings at the Opera House in the Haymarket. Then he announced two evening meetings: one at the Opera House, the other at Bow Common where he could reach another class of people.

A much poorer class of people lived near Bow Common, but Dwight yearned to reach them too. With the sawdust floor, galvanized iron roof, and gaslight shining on the faces of the ragged, unkempt people at Bow Common, Dwight felt right at home—like he was back in Illinois Street preaching to the people he loved best!

Each night Dwight would preach at 7:30 to roughly eight or nine thousand at Bow Common. Then at 8:30, he and Sankey jumped into a brougham, trotting as swiftly as traffic allowed up the Mile-End Road and through the city, under shored-up Temple Bar, and around Trafalgar Square to the Haymarket: they would traverse from the East End to the West End, from a world of slums and squalor to that of great mansions and the royal parks, from dock workers to duchesses.

Dwight's flexibility in preaching to two very different sorts of crowds impressed an attending aristocrat:

"Nothing showed the wonderful adaptability of Mr. Moody more than his coming from Bow Road, the poorest part of the East End, to the very antipodes of it all in character and surroundings, and yet at once hitting on the right note of dealing with the new conditions." Near the Opera House were St. James, Mayfair, Westminster, Belgravia, and the heart of fashionable London.

One eyewitness marveled at what he witnessed at the Haymarket site nightly: "The scene in the Haymarket baffles description. It was literally blocked with the carriages of the aristocratic and plutocratic of the land; and the struggle for admission was perhaps even more severe in the West than in the East."

Another participant expressed amazement at the good acoustics in the Opera House: "When we got to the Opera House, we found an immense crowd outside; but we got a place at the very top of the highest gallery, and although at that distance Mr. Moody seemed a tiny figure of a man, every word, even his whispered words, were heard. I was struck with the impression which Mr. Sankey's singing made on the audience."

Opening the campaign at the Opera House turned out to be an excellent idea, for it insured that even aristocratic people could attend. In fact, one of Dwight's staunch supporters turned out to be the duchess of Sutherland who "insisted on going every day." The Sutherlands had entertained Dwight at Dunrobin Castle in the Highlands where the duchess was a countess in her own right as well as a chieftain. The duke, according to common knowledge, owned more acres than any man in Europe.

The duke expressed his thanks for Dwight's ministry

149

in a letter where he told him, "God bless you. I shall never forget what I have heard from you. If you knew what a life mine is, in ways I was not able to tell you the other day, and what a terrible story mine has been, you would pray for me much." In a subsequent, more positive letter, the duke thanked Dwight "for all the joy and strength our dear Lord has given me through you, and I pray that your wonderful work may be more and more blessed."

In her enthusiasm for Dwight's meetings, the duchess would collect numerous friends and relatives at palatial Stafford House and whisk them in her carriage along Pall Mall to the Haymarket. Some of them objected to it: "The mixture of religious fervor and the most intense toadyism of the duchess was horribly disgusting," said Lady Barker with considerable disdain.

The Princess of Wales, thirty-year-old Alexandra, entered the royal box at one of the early Bible readings. When he realized who she was, Sankey burst into the backstage room, his eyes popping, and his hands nervously straightening bow tie and whiskers.

"Moody, the Princess of Wales has just arrived!"

Dwight, occupied in talking with a young English helper, looked up. "May she be blessed. I'll be out in a minute. Now, Inglis, as I was saying."

The young Englishman noted the difference between the two men. Sankey, he observed, was "all in a flutter," while "Moody takes it as a matter of course. When we came out on the platform, I watched them. Mr. Moody rolled into his chair like a New England farmer. There he stood with a tweed suit on, pockets full of papers, and said in his usual way, 'Hymn number so-and-so, let's all rise and sing it.' "

Princess Alexandra attended the meetings two or three times and told one of her friends that Dwight's ministry had been a definite help to her. On the strength of reports such as this one, the dowager countess of Gainsborough decided to write Queen Victoria.

Her letter suggested that Her Majesty would like at least once to hear the American evangelists "who are so occupying men's minds at this time—& drawing such crowds to hear them." The dowager countess mentioned the "Royal box which Your Majesty could go to privately."

Queen Victoria responded saying that she did not go to large public places anymore. Aside from that, the Queen thought Moody and Sankey must be "good and sincere people," but their meetings were not "the sort of religious performance which I like. This sensational style of excitement like the Revivals is not the religion which can last, and is not, I think, wholesome for the mind or heart, though there may be instances where it does good."

Concluding her rather barbed letter, the Queen expressed her opinion that the best kind of preaching is "eloquent, simple preaching, with plain practical teaching" which is "far more likely to do real and permanent good, and this can surely be heard in all Protestant Churches, whether in the Established Church or amongst Dissenters, if the Ministers are thoroughly earnest."

After preaching to huge crowds gathered at Bow Common and the Opera House, and even schoolboys at Eton—although Dwight and Sankey nearly had eggs tossed at them there—they were ready to travel back to

America and see their friends and loved ones again.

They had arrived in England on June 17, 1873, and were scheduled to leave on the SS *Spain* on August 4, 1875. The attendance at the meetings in London's centers alone totaled 2,330,000. Scotland, Ireland, and England would never be the same. Much of the evangelistic mission work started as a direct result of the Moody campaign and continued under the able hands of local laymen and ministers.

Headed back to America after a two-year absence, Dwight and Sankey wondered, *What does the future hold for us there?*

seventeen

Northfield Revisited

M oody and Sankey had left New York in obscurity; they returned on August 14, 1875, international celebrities. Critics such as the *New York Times* still asserted they had been sent to England by showman P. T. Barnum. But an elderly London minister's remark indicated what lay ahead for the two in their own country: "America had heard with shock how they were run after. They owe their success partly to their cheek, partly to their music."

A bevy of reporters surrounded the Moody and Sankey families, wanting to know their plans. Characteristically, Dwight would say nothing of the future except, "I am going right up to Northfield, Massachusetts, to see my mother." His whirlwind campaigns had left little time for correspondence, and he was eager to hear about his family and news of home.

Reaching Northfield on August 16, Dwight, Emma, and the children found Dwight's brother George waiting for them in an old, dilapidated buggy drawn by a plodding farm horse. Samuel followed in a wagon with their baggage.

Dwight breathed the still August air deeply. Excitedly, he remarked to Emma, drowsy from their long journey, "Isn't it wonderful to come back here? How I have missed

Northfield! There's not another place on earth like it!" If Emma thought otherwise, she kept her thoughts to herself.

The entourage wound slowly over the narrow Connecticut River by the railroad toll bridge, up the hill into the avenue of majestic elms arrayed in summer splendor, and on to Betsey's little white house.

Seventy-year-old Betsey, demure in her dainty white widow's cap, stood in the doorway, waiting for her son. She had pride in Dwight. She had heard about the huge crowds that came to hear him in Scotland and Ireland and England, even dukes and duchesses and other fine lords and ladies. She didn't understand why they would come—she still did not approve of what Dwight preached.

As Dwight hugged his mother, she clung to him with a strength that surprised him. He realized at that moment how much his mother loved him. He wished he could stay nearby. She needed to have her family around her, not scattered across the country.

Somehow they all squeezed themselves into the small frame house that already contained Betsey and the unmarried brothers Edwin and Samuel. How happy Dwight was to be home with his family—especially with his brother Samuel. Samuel's personality endeared him to people, despite the fact that he was the town tax collector. His slight frame combined with chronic epilepsy made him seem vulnerable, and most of the town people reached out to him.

The days at Northfield refreshed Dwight. He and Samuel climbed the surrounding hills and drove in the buggy along old familiar lanes. He remembered all the pleasant scenes of his childhood: where he had picked berries, pastured cows, and gathered chestnuts.

Dwight hoped to spend his days at Northfield exercising his body and soul. He knew his body badly needed exercise; he had had so little time to exercise while he was overseas!

But his soul needed refreshing too. Dwight yearned to spend hours just studying the Bible and meditating on what God said in His Word.

Although he had intended simply to rest during his stay at Northfield, the Unitarian minister of First Parish Church invited him to speak. But Dwight refused, saying to himself: "Those who believe in Unitarianism insult Christ, and whoever insults Christ insults me."

But Dwight's heart burned for his family, cousins, neighbors, and the whole community—all "cold Unitarians"—to be drawn to Christ. So grudgingly, the Orthodox, Trinitarian minister, T. J. Clark, agreed to an extra service in Second Parish Church on Sunday afternoon, September 5.

Everybody in the community came—even Betsey, whose pride in her famous son overrode her Unitarian convictions. Samuel came, too—perhaps as much out of curiosity as anything else. He chuckled over Dwight's "revivalist tendencies."

Before long, the church literally bulged; the underpinning was giving way! George Moody strode up the aisle as the people sang hymns prompted by Dwight. George whispered in Dwight's ear, and at the end of the verse, Dwight lifted his hand. In a casual tone but with a broad smile on his face, he announced: "The place is full. Many are still outside. I'll preach on the steps so all can hear. While we sing the next number all will go out, beginning at the rear."

The people sat around on the grass and in the dusty street, and a small boy wriggled up an apple tree. Only when some saw the old white building sagging dangerously did they understood Dwight's skill in emptying the church swiftly and averting sudden panic. The deacons shored the building up before the next meeting!

Sankey perched his little harmonium on the narrow covered platform designed for churchgoers to step off wagons without getting their feet wet and began singing "The Ninety and Nine." Incredibly, on that quiet summer afternoon, the slight breeze carried Sankey's words and song across and down the Connecticut River about a mile where they were heard by a Mr. Caldwell. He had refused in anger to go to the service but was sitting on his porch and listened to every distinct word. The words stirred his conscience and led to his conversion.

Dwight preached about Zaccheus, and the Northfield town folks never forgot that unusual Sunday afternoon. Seventy years later, W. T. Holton, the son of Dwight's first cousin Jonathan, who farmed across the Connecticut River, could remember the details. "The sun shining over the distant hills from the far side of the river; the air, so calm that not a leaf stirred; not a sound to disturb the quiet except the low murmur of voices from little groups as they discussed in subdued tones the meeting and sermon. The familiar surroundings of the town and the faces of the neighbors were only a little more real than the scenes that had been vividly portrayed by the speaker."

People from nearby communities swarmed into Northfield to glimpse the famous evangelists. Special trains arrived from Brattleboro, Vermont, and converged upon the Orthodox Church. Betsey, too, and other family members, including Samuel, continued to come to the meetings.

There was opposition, especially from the town blacksmith. Dwight said the blacksmith "hated me, spoke most bitterly against me. The smithy was the rendezvous of all the strong opposition men."

So Dwight prayed and wrestled with God for his family, his loved ones, his townspeople. Above all, his heart nearly burst for his mother to know the Savior. Perhaps some song, some graphic Bible story would pierce her shield of moral confidence. But she gave no indication of any inner stirrings until one of the last evenings when Dwight invited those to rise in their places who wished to acknowledge Christ as the Son of God and trust in Him as Savior, "that we might pray for you." Betsy stood up. Dwight was so overcome that he could barely ask one of the others to lead in prayer.

On the last night, Samuel stood.

Samuel's conversion was solid. Like a river that had been dammed, a torrent of love began to pour through him. From then on, he took a leading part in religious meetings. He would go out and talk with weak brothers and help them to their feet. Like his older brother, Samuel would search for souls on both sides of the Connecticut River, in both sides of the valley. When

Northfield formed a YMCA, they elected him president.

Following Dwight's preaching in Northfield, it became a center of "the greatest revival ever known in that part of the state," according to W. T. Holton. Prayer meetings were held in schoolhouses and private homes, and active workers, speakers, and singers alike would travel around spreading the Gospel.

The acceptance and love Dwight received from his hometown and family and their new interest in his work caused him to realize that he needed to put down roots.

He had not really considered putting them down in Northfield. Then his mother's chickens kept crossing over to a neighbor's corn field—much to the neighbor's annoyance. Dwight had to make things right with the neighbor, so he approached him.

Dwight stopped his buggy and told the neighbor, Elisha Alexander, "I want to buy a strip of that field."

Elisha responded, "No. I don't care to sell unless it's the whole place."

"How many acres?"

"Twelve."

"How much?" Dwight asked.

"Well, I'll take thirty-five hundred dollars for the whole place with house and barns."

"I'll take it!"

It just happened that some money had recently been sent to Dwight as a gift, so he was able to pay the entire amount. He was now the proud owner of a house in Northfield.

At the time, Dwight could scarcely know what lay

ahead for him and his modest purchase. Just now, he needed to get back to business—but in New York, not Chicago.

eighteen

American Triumph

D uring their stay at Northfield, Dwight and
Sankey made plans for their future campaigns.
Dwight desired to reach America for Christ—
but would America receive him and his message? "Water
runs downhill and the highest hills are the great cities,"
said Dwight. "If we can stir them we shall stir the whole
country."

Others also wondered if the evangelistic team would
be effective in their own land. Many of the New York
newspapers expressed skepticism, and the famous
Brooklyn preacher DeWitt Talmage had wondered
whether his weekly journal should support or discourage
the meetings.

America needed a religious awakening. The wounds
created by the Civil War a mere decade past had not
totally healed. In the North, an obsession with money
prevailed; while in the South, reconstruction had failed
and people struggled in the midst of poor living conditions. Numerous immigrants had also altered the texture
of the nation. And most Americans whether newcomers
or those with deep roots, looked to some technological
utopia and cast aside old moralities.

Dwight had reluctantly decided not to start in Chicago
because he was afraid the ministers would not come
together to support him. Instead, he chose Brooklyn as

his jumping-off place, much to the chagrin of numerous pessimists. His detractors were bewildered when an overflow crowd of between twelve- and twenty-thousand people pressed into and around the rink on Clermont Avenue to hear him.

Streetcar companies had laid extra tracks to the building, and at the close of the service thousands had to walk to their homes because of the many extra passengers on the cars. Dwight wrote Farwell in Chicago, "Pray daily for me. I never needed the help of my friends as much as now."

Some of these detractors soon had to admit that Dwight had held some of the largest assemblies in America in rapt attention. Of course Dwight realized that some people came out of curiosity, but the Lord could still reach them. After a month's duration, when the Brooklyn meetings closed, Dwight's heart was heavy because of vast numbers of still unreached, unchurched people living there. But the Brooklyn meetings launched him with a bang and proved that clergy would unite "zealously and harmoniously and intelligently to carry on the work."

Dwight and Sankey went from Brooklyn to Philadelphia in November 1875. Great preparation had taken place for the mission, and John Wanamaker, a good friend of Dwight's, had bought the old freight depot of the Pennsylvania Railroad, completely refitting it and offering it rent free for the campaign.

One hundred eighty ministers of every denomination had signed the invitation for Dwight to come and worked diligently to make the campaign a success. A Philadelphian who attended wrote to an English friend about the meetings, telling him, "The doors open about 1 ½ hours before the time and it takes about 10 minutes to fill with at least 12,000 persons. It is wonderful."

Every Friday Dwight held special meetings for alcoholics. He also had women's meetings, but as in Scotland and England, his delight was in the young men's meetings. He wrote his friend Henry Drummond in Scotland on December 4: "The work among young men in this country is growing splendidly. I am glad I went to England to learn how to reach young men. Could you come over and help us? I think you would get a few thousand souls on these shores if you should come. I miss you more than I can tell, you do not know how much I want you with me." Drummond, still a college student, declined to interrupt his studies this time, although he and Dwight were very close, and he loved to work with him.

Princeton University issued Dwight a "special request" to come for a day, which he gladly did. Dwight said later, "I have not seen anything in America that pleased me like what I have seen in Princeton. They have got a Holy Ghost revival there. The President of the college told me he had never seen anything like it in Princeton."

Working in Philadelphia, Dwight showed himself to be the same unaffected, integrated personality his friends in Britain had known. As usual, he was utterly absorbed in his work. One of his Chicago church officers came to the platform at the close of an evening service as the inquiry meeting began. "I touched Mr. Sankey on the shoulder, and he did the undignified thing of embracing me," he said. "After a little conversation with him I went to

162

where Moody was, and touched him on the shoulder also, when he turned and quickly and earnestly said, 'Talk to that woman!' "

President Grant and several of his Cabinet, visiting Philadelphia for the Centennial Exhibition, sat on the platform on Sunday, January 19, 1876. Dwight made no attempt to be introduced afterwards; he had a bad cold and a hoarse voice but even if well would not have sought out the president.

Even as a serious evangelist, Dwight retained his playful side. He and his family stayed at the Wanamaker mansion during the Philadelphia campaign, and when his work was over for the day or evening, he had the ability to relax in a moment. One of the Wanamaker children said of him: "The thing I remember most was Mr. Moody and father playing bears with us children. Such wild exciting times as we had. They would get down on all fours and chase us. We would shriek and scream and run. It was pandemonium!"

The end of January 1876, brought a close to the Philadelphia campaign. Dwight and Sankey traveled to New York to begin a long-awaited series of meetings. Dwight arrived just a day before the campaign was to open, but he had let the committee of laymen and ministers know exactly what should be done, and they had organized it with true New York business skill. The treasurer, J. Pierpont Morgan, was the same age as Dwight; and thirty-two-year-old Cornelius Vanderbilt, Jr., was one of the private guarantors who advanced money against expenses.

The committee had leased Barnum's "Great Roman

Hippodrome" which stood on Madison Avenue, the future site of Madison Square Garden. The Hippodrome provided the dividing line between the very wealthy and the very poor. On the one side, said an observer, "lie the homes of wealth, the avenues of fashion, and the great hotels; on the other, the masses of the middle class and, a little beyond, the crowded abodes of the poor and the dens of wretchedness and vice." Dwight's heart always went out to the poor, but he also saw the same spiritual needs in the very rich.

The campaign chairman, William E. Dodge, informed a friend: "We are fitting up two large halls opening into each other; one, holding about eight or nine thousand and the other about six thousand." They had allowed for inquiry rooms, and an up-to-date touch was an internal electric telegraph whereby orders could be sent to regulate lighting, heating, and ventilation.

A thousand-voice choir led a song service for a half hour before the little door opened behind the wide platform and Dwight Moody stepped on stage. An onlooker said that Dwight seemed "to cover the space between the door and the pulpit in one step! Mr. Moody was a meteor. He was at the little railing in front, his hand raised, our heads bowed in prayer and we all saying 'Amen' almost before we knew it. How lithe, springy and buoyant he was. How full of life and spirit!"

Dwight's weight was still mostly muscle and bone, not fat. Since he had no time for open-air exercise, he used a health-lift every day to try to stay somewhat fit. The papers described Dwight as "short, stout-built, square shouldered with bullet-shaped head set close on the shoulders, black eyes that twinkle merrily at times, and a full but not heavy beard and moustache."

New Yorkers responded enthusiastically to the meetings. The chairman, Mr. Dodge, wrote an English friend: "Nothing has ever reached our great masses of non-church-going people as these meetings have. Our ministers have been warmed and helped, cold Christians restored, and many careless persons brought to Christ. I do not think the work has been truer or larger in any place Mr. Moody has visited. He is staying with me and I find his cheery whole-souled humble consecration a great spur and help."

Dwight preached the same message as in England but adapted to his American audience. Even though he knew his calling was to be an evangelist to the masses, he relished dealing with individuals in the inquiry room. He had long outgrown the habit of tossing off Scripture texts to an inquirer; instead, "His questionings speedily determined whether an inquirer was sincere and genuine, or hypocritical and evasive. With astonishing rapidity he could turn a man mentally and morally inside out, expose his fallacies, moral inconsistencies, perversions, willfulness and alienation from God." He desired that lay people "learn the art of personally winning souls."

At the campaign's close, even the *New York Times* conceded that "the work accomplished this winter by Mr. Moody in this city for private and public morals will live. The drunken have become sober, the vicious virtuous, the worldly and self-seeking unselfish, the ignoble noble, and the impure pure. A new hope has lifted up hundreds of human beings, a new consolation has come to the sorrowful, and a better principle has entered the sordid life of the day, through the labors of these plain men."

A troubling incident bothered Dwight at the end of the New York campaign. Several ministers left on vacation, and Dwight was distressed, thinking they should have been as interested in conversion in New York as he was. He made a terrible mistake in one of his Bible readings when he lashed out at the New York *Ledger,* the society gossip paper to which several fashionable ministers contributed. Even Dr. Hall, the meeting chairman, was a staunch supporter. Dwight said later that, "I didn't mean to say anything against the paper but somehow it popped up." The moment he finished preaching he turned to apologize, but Dr. Hall had left the chair in a huff and did not see Dwight again for some time.

The incident caused Dwight to close the Hippodrome mission two weeks before the assigned three months were up. Almost at once, he realized he had done the wrong thing. He realized that in closing the meeting early, "I grieved the Holy Spirit." In spite of his mistake, Dwight never looked back with regret; he always looked ahead and retained an effervescent optimism.

Emma and the children had already left for Augusta, Georgia, because the New York weather had been too hard on young Willie. Their friend, D. W. Whittle, was holding a mission there, and Dwight soon joined them. Although Dwight came to Augusta to rest, he soon involved himself in Whittle's work. Whittle fought a slight temptation to resent his intrusion. But he calmed himself as he thought, *I have considered that Moody is a mighty man of God, the*

Whitefield of this century, owned and honored of God, and if he has been led of God to come here and speak it is a very petty spirit that would think of self in connection with the work.

Whittle's understanding of Dwight paid off. Dwight took him into his confidence as they walked along the banks of the Savannah River in the spring sunshine. "I don't know that I will ever go to England again," Dwight said. "I am entirely bankrupt as to sermons and material —I have used up everything. I'm going to study and make new sermons but I think it will be three or four years before I shall go—if I ever go. You and Bliss had better wait until next year before going, and you must study all you can."

Dwight felt empty—and spiritually bankrupt, as he put it. At the pinnacle of his influence in the United States, he stood in danger of spiritual burn-out.

Not requiring much sleep, Dwight would rise early to read his Bible and pray, and he had the unique ability to catnap anytime of the day or night. His original filing system consisted of using a large envelope for each sermon. Then he would put a scrawled sheet of headings and notes and stories clipped from papers or jotted on paper for illustrations. He would label each envelope with the place and date of each delivery. This method enabled Dwight's sermons to be fresh. He might preach on the same topic, but he would vary it each time.

He also worried about divisions, jealousies—everything that hindered the cause of Christ. His desire was that Christians, especially ministers of the Gospel, would put aside their differences and work together. It always saddened Dwight when a minister or leading Christian got caught in a scandal, and he made it a policy not to repeat any gossip or hearsay that could damage the cause of Christ.

When it was alleged that a leading minister had committed adultery, Dwight's comment was "I hope if he is guilty, it will never be known, it would have an awful effect." However, Whittle also knew that if it fell Dwight's lot to deliver such a person to justice once the truth were known, he would not fail to do so.

At that time, Dwight's influence in the country was enormous. In fact, Farwell advised Cyrus McCormick who thought of running for vice president in June of 1876, that five-thousand dollars given to Moody's cause in Chicago and widely advertised would do more "than all the money you could put into the hands of political wire-pullers."

But Dwight's opinion of himself continued to be an honest, humble one. On one occasion, he told reporters, "I am the most overestimated man in America." He thought of himself simply as "the mouthpiece and expression of a deep and mysterious wave of religious feeling now passing over the nation. The disasters and disappointments of the year, the reaction against the skepticism and selfish greed of the day have prepared the minds of the people for a profound religious transformation or impulse." Nevertheless, everyone in the country, whether in log cabins of the Appalachians, in frontier wagons in some remote Montana valley, or in the soot and grime of Detroit or Pittsburgh, knew and loved Dwight Moody and Ira Sankey.

Another problem the two had to contend with were imitators. "Moody and Sankey meetings are advertised, at which Moody's sermons will be read, Moody and Sankey Hymnbooks used, then somebody dashes out like Brother Moody, or tries to sing a solo like Brother Sankey," complained a New York Methodist minister.

Moody and Sankey also had to deal with exploiters. "Perhaps you noticed," Dwight told one audience, "that there is someone at the door selling photographs of Mr. Sankey and myself. I want to say that this is one of the thorns we have in the flesh. Those are no more photographs of Mr. Sankey and myself than they are of you or anyone else." With press photography in its infancy, only people who attended the meetings could know what they looked like. And no one could photograph them unless they consented and sat still.

Exasperated, Dwight added that they had tried to stop these people legally but "couldn't do it. And now we ask you, if you have any regard for us, not to patronize them. I hope I will never have to refer to it again, for I always feel like a fool when I have to talk about myself."

Leaving Augusta, the Moodys and Whittles stopped in Atlanta, then went on to Chattanooga where Dwight spoke to a large gathering. On the way, Whittle enjoyed pointing out various battlefields and fortifications as they "reversed" Sherman's March to the Sea.

The rest of May, Dwight preached all over the Midwest: Nashville, St. Louis, Kansas, Omaha, and even in Council Bluffs, Iowa. At one of the meetings in St. Louis, a stranger to the area, James G. Butler, wandered into an after-meeting. Butler said that Dwight "came down where I was sitting, and said: 'Are you a Christian?' "

"'Yes, sir!' I replied, rather expecting he would say something courteous and cordial. But, no. He only said, pointing to another man just across: 'Talk to that man about his soul.' I did. There was just nothing else for me to do. If the man was blessed as I was, he is a happy man today."

At Des Moines, the ministers had decided to cancel all Sunday services and tell their congregations to attend Moody's meetings at the campaign headquarters. However, F. G. Ensign, Dwight's friend from the previous decade, warned them he would not approve.

When a determined group met Dwight on arrival, they told him their plans for the meeting. "Mr. Moody, we have decided, our association has voted, that we will not have any services on Sunday. We want all our people to go to the rink at 10:30."

"No, I can't do that," Dwight protested.

"But we have decided it," committee members declared.

"I can't do it! You will have to have your church services. You must have your church services, and then at 2:30 so as not to interfere with the services we have the meeting in the rink."

Dwight admitted to a friend: "I have often to do a shabby thing. A committee takes a great deal of trouble about something, I see it will not suit, so I cut discussion short by saying I am going to do it another way. It is very mean of me, but would take a tremendous time in committee and I have to do it."

Sometimes his brusqueness offended others. Whittle said that Dwight's reception of a campaign committee was based on his ability to turn a situation around and have them think his idea was theirs: "About fifteen persons of the committee have been grieved because Moody has ignored them and gone ahead with meetings as he pleased. He keeps quiet, drawing out in full all the complaints and injured feelings and then explains and rights everything, suggesting what he thinks best and drawing out the ministers to adopt it as from themselves."

As the Midwest evangelistic tour came to a close, Dwight was again nominated to be president of the Illinois State Sunday School Association, which he presided over for their four-day conference at Jacksonville, Illinois. Sankey remained with him, but he was quite ill by the time they finally returned to Chicago after three years of travel.

Dwight had come to a crossroad in his life. Where would he put down permanent roots? Would he put them down in Chicago or in Northfield? He loved both places—and his family badly needed a place to settle down. Much depended on his making the right choice, but for the moment he was in a quandary as to which decision was best.

nineteen

The Crossroad

*D*wight loved the Chicago church. After all, he had poured himself into building it, soliciting funds for its maintenance, and then preaching in it for years. He referred to the church as his "first love." He shared with Farwell that he would seldom "get on my knees in private but I think and pray for the dear church in Chicago." When one of the deacons had visited him in Philadelphia, he'd spent two hours going over the church membership roll and asking in detail how each person was doing.

The new church building stood on the Chicago Avenue site he had secured before leaving for Europe. Although the church was still in debt, when he returned he made a few successful calls for funds and cleared the indebtedness. Thus on June 1, 1876, despite a pouring rain, the church was opened and Dwight preached. The church was formally dedicated on July 16.

Dwight thought it strange to be back in Chicago—it had changed so much in the three years he had been gone. The surroundings he had known and loved were altered beyond recognition by rebuilding, yet were still smoky from the fire. The stockyard stench traveled everywhere, blanketing much of Chicago with its own peculiar aroma. But the crowds of people and the multitudes of ragged, dirty children remained the same. Dwight longed to reach out to them again with Christ's love. He sensed, too, that not only had Chicago changed, but he had changed.

On the spur of the moment he decided to accept the Chicago campaign invitation first, then the one in Boston. He even allowed himself to get back somewhat into the solicitation of funds to erect a temporary tabernacle. Farwell said no one would give to it, but then changed his mind when he realized the building could be salvaged later as a permanent building.

Prior to starting in Chicago, Dwight and his family returned to Northfield for a couple of summer months. They could enjoy their very own home, which delighted the whole family. Emma had much to do in Northfield for, as she wrote Jane Mackinnon in Scotland on September 11, "We are in our own home, and though in a most delightful spot with such beautiful scenery, it is a place where it is very difficult to get servants, and I have had to act in all sorts of capacities. We have had company every day since we came into our house, and it has been a pleasure to my husband and myself, but I found my husband's urgent letters took most all my spare time."

An ugly rumor in the British papers saying Moody and Sankey had quarreled over money in New York slightly spoiled this time of leisure. As Emma assured Jane: "The whole thing is a wicked fabrication. Mr. Sankey and Mr. Moody have never quarreled about anything. I have not seen anything from the newspapers trouble Mr. Moody as this has done."

Reveling in being with Sam, Dwight drove around

173

Northfield with him and listened to his wonderful plans for Northfield. His plans included the spiritual and temporal welfare of the community. And Dwight's excitement concerning all the possibilities for his hometown knew no bounds.

Before long, the family returned to Chicago, arriving there on September 30. This time, they stayed with Emma's sister and her husband, the Holdens.

Six thousand Sunday school teachers, five hundred singers, and a hundred ministers, filled the tabernacle at eight o'clock on Sunday morning. Following hymns, prayer, Scripture reading, and Sankey's solos, Dwight began to preach the sermon "Rolling away the Stone."

Whittle thought his talk was "as earnest, plain, simple, and practical and as absent from all self-consciousness as if delivered to his own Sunday school teachers. You are interested and inspired, and think he has just begun when he stops as abruptly as he began, offers prayer, pronounces the benediction and the meeting is over."

It seemed this campaign would proceed like any other. The first Sunday afternoon service was packed out, and with each subsequent service, thousands were turned away. Forgetting the "Crazy Moody" of old, Chicago now raved over its own world-renowned evangelist.

The Chicago Omnibus Company arranged for extra buses, timing each bus so it could connect with the tram cars. A theology professor who witnessed the crowds expressed puzzlement over Dwight's campaign: "It is perfectly astounding to me that a man with so little training should have come to understand the public so well. He cannot read the Greek Testament; indeed he has difficulty with parts of it in the English version, but he excels any man I ever heard in making his hearers see the point of a text of Scripture."

Whittle had dinner with Dwight on Thursday during the first week. He found Dwight unusually solemn and concerned with God trying him. He said he could pray, "'O God, search me,' but when it comes to asking God to 'try me' it's a solemn thing. I don't know as I could stand trying. Am I ready to be laid aside from my work, to be tried? Am I ready to meet affliction?"

The next day, Friday, October 6, Whittle again dined with Dwight and found him still obsessed with the thought of God "trying him." Later that evening, Dwight had invited the officers of the Chicago Avenue Church to have tea with him at Brevoort House before the meeting. Whittle came in late, bringing a stack of Dwight's letters and one telegram being held for him at the YMCA. He handed the stack to Dwight, who began opening the telegram. "While sitting at the table he read it and gave a cry of pain, stood upon his feet and said, 'Sam is dead,' and sat down with his head buried in his hands to cry," Whittle recalled. "In a few minutes he said, 'Whittle, you will have to take the meeting tonight. I cannot be with you longer,' and went out."

When Whittle reached the tabernacle later in the evening, he found Dwight talking with the ministers. He was going east to bury his brother, and the committee unanimously asked Whittle to take over the meetings.

As Dwight journeyed on the train and wept from sorrow, his thoughts revolved around his family: "Oh, how deep the sorrow! The dear boy was gone for ever."

Samuel, for whom he had prayed twenty years, who at the last "took a stand for Christ, and went to work, zealous work," was gone. As the train rumbled through Indiana into Ohio, Dwight wept and wept again until heaven's voice "at last made itself heard to my heart: 'Thy brother shall rise again.' The cloud was lifted, and for about 500 miles on my way to my home that verse rang in my ears."

Samuel's death gave Dwight a desire to do all that Samuel had longed to do for Northfield. But Dwight was needed in Chicago. He loved both places. He wrote to the pastor of Chicago Avenue, W. J. Erdman, "I do hope you will hold the people to the thought of love. I am sure that is where the churches have all gone astray. We must have it above all things."

The Chicago campaign forged ahead from 1876 into 1877. For a Presbyterian minister who took part, it was a turning point: "That wonderful revival. That tremendous audience, and its voice in song like the voice of the ocean. The mighty faith and courage of the undertaking. Think what it required to prepare for an audience of ten thousand people, and what failure, in the presence of such vast preparation, would mean!"

As the campaign reached its closing weeks, Dwight still faced a dilemma: where should he put down roots? Another question also nagged at his soul: would he burn out in a few more years?

During the course of the campaign Dwight had faced a number of tragedies: the death of his brother, Sam, and a dangerous attack of scarlet fever for twelve-year-old Emma. Also, although she did not tell Dwight, his wife, Emma, was told by her doctor that her heart was diseased and in critical condition.

Another blow to Dwight came with the sudden death of Philip Bliss, who Dwight said was like his hymns, "full of faith and cheer—in all the years I have known and worked with him I have never seen him cast down." Bliss was riding on the Pacific Express near Ashtabula, Ohio, when an iron bridge gave way in a snowstorm, and the train plunged seventy feet down to a frozen creek and caught fire. Over a hundred people died, but amazingly, Bliss crawled from the wreckage, then went back to free his wife. But not a remnant of either of them could ever be identified. These sorrows made Dwight, according to Whittle, "very kind and tender."

In spite of the tragedies, Dwight still had work to do. On January 28, 1877, a week before his fortieth birthday, the Boston campaign began. If Dwight failed in Boston, it would be the death knell to his influence in America. However, when he finished there on the first of May, he had received a new vision.

Some of those opposed to Dwight and his campaign included Unitarians, liberal intellectuals, and Irish Catholics. However, his friends were led by the Reverend A. J. Gordon, the saintly pastor of Clarendon Street. Few of Dwight's boyhood friends remained; Edward Kimball had moved to California, and Dwight's Holton uncles had retired.

A tabernacle had been specially built for the campaign, with over ninety churches participating. Though the building seated only six thousand, Dwight and Sankey considered it one of the most pleasant places in which they had ministered.

"Christianity," Dwight exclaimed the first night, "has been on the defensive long enough, specially here in New England. The time's come f'r us to open a war of aggression. Remember during the War of the Rebellion some of the generals kept their armies on the defensive until they got confusticated? I guess a good many Christians here in New England have just got into their cushioned pews and gone to sleep." Dwight got their attention with these opening remarks!

Then he urged a course of action. Christians needed to "wake up and move forward in solid columns." And they should not be defensive, but aggressive: "These drinking shops 'n' billiard halls 'n' gambling dens should be visited 'n' told of Christ 'n' heaven 'n' if they won't come to the tabernacle 'n' hear the Gospel, let us go to their houses 'n' preach the Gospel to them 'n' it won't be long before hundreds are reached."

Many of Boston's newspapers took a positive approach to the campaign, and the weekday papers, in particular, gave it much space. The *Globe* actually recovered from financial disaster by printing ample coverage of the campaign.

Even Walt Whitman, the well-known American poet, got into the act. But his poetic remarks tended to be disparaging, particularly in a final stanza:

> *I Walt tell him he is an ignorant charlatan,*
> *a mistaken enthusiast, and that Boston*
> *will ere long desire him to git.*

However, Boston did not desire him to "git." Not even

cultured Bostonians. A telling indication of Dwight's popularity occurred when the Thomas Orchestra gave a benefit for the "Old South" fund and played to a half-empty hall. The same night over six thousand people crowded into the tabernacle to hear Moody and Sankey.

So successful was the Boston campaign as far as Dwight and Sankey were concerned, that they ranked it alongside the Edinburgh campaign. Among the wonderful new friends Dwight came to know during the Boston meetings was Phillips Brooks, the author of "O Little Town of Bethlehem." Brooks, an Episcopal minister, preached during Dwight's absence one night.

As usual, at the close of the campaign, Dwight held a two-day Christian Convention. He also tried to gain entrance to Harvard but failed. He advocated temperance, holding a Temperance Conference, and brought Frances Willard as a leader of evangelism for women. She was well known for her stand on temperance, and Dwight wanted her to sit on the campaign platform; she refused saying she would not sit with Unitarians.

For Dwight, however, the future seemed not to be reckoned by sinners saved or drunks redeemed. Throughout the campaign, he stayed with Henry Fowle Durant, the founder of Wellesley College for girls. When Durant talked about the ideas implemented in his college, Dwight listened carefully. Durant's vision for Wellesley seemed to echo Samuel's dreams for Northfield that he had shared with Dwight the summer before he died.

twenty

The Educator

During Sam's last summer, the two brothers had taken the buggy to look at cattle near Warwick. Sam was a library patron, had founded a debating club, and was outspoken at town meetings on Northfield's lack of good education—especially for girls such as his twin sister. As leader of the local YMCA and a lay evangelist making amends for twenty years of antagonism toward Christianity, his hopes and dreams for Northfield now blended with Dwight's.

On their return trip past a mountain lane, the brothers found a crippled, frail man standing in front of his cabin door and stopped to chat with him. He had been reading the Greek New Testament to his young daughters as they braided straw hats to earn a living. A pile of well-worn books—Thomas à Kempis, Madame Guyon, John Bunyan, and others—were stacked close to Horace Parmelee Sikes's position on his couch.

Dwight asked him, "Where have you taken your education? How do you get along?"

Sikes replied: "I went to Oberlin College for four years in the 1840s and attended Wilbraham College some. I taught for awhile at a good school, but then became paralyzed and had to quit." Sikes lamented that his daughters, Jennie and Julia, could not hope to have a similar education. Smiling, he said, "We don't have much roast turkey or plum pudding, but we get along!"

Mrs. Sikes stepped in just then, wiping soapsuds from her hands, "We just have to take things right out of the hand of God."

One of the girls added happily, "But we have a real home!"

As Sam and Dwight drove home, they discussed the Sikes's plight. Mr. Sikes could teach his daughters Greek, but what future could they have with no education beyond that and the little district school in the hills? They could not pay board for the girls to attend the public high school at Greenfield. The girls' future could only hold a life of married drudgery on a mountain farm or as factory hands.

Sam said, "I tell you, Dwight, we've got to have a girls' school in Northfield! Not only for my sister to attend, but for all the girls like Jennie and Julia Sikes. Otherwise their lives will be wasted!"

Dwight responded with a nod. Deep in thought, they continued home in silence.

Now with Sam gone, his dream became a sacred trust for Dwight. He might never have done anything toward its fulfilment had he not been a guest of Henry Fowle Durant at Boston during the first part of 1877.

Durant, a prominent wealthy Boston lawyer, had retired from law to devote himself to Christian causes after the death of his only son. Dwight considered him one of my "old friends and one that stood by me in days before I was much known. All through the Boston work he was with me every night, and did a great work."

Durant had opened Wellesley College on part of his estate in the northwestern section of Boston. He wanted Wellesley to be a first-class college where girls of moderate means might receive "opportunities for education equivalent to those offered at Harvard." Durant had also adopted the idea from Mount Holyoke Seminary that every girl should do a regular share of domestic service. He said he did not want "velvet girls" but "calico girls." The fees charged were $250 a year, or half the cost, the other half being made up by the college. Durant also required every teacher to possess not only academic skill but what he termed "vital Christianity," and Bible training became part of the compulsory requirements.

Dwight's stay with Durant crystallized his determination to organize a preparatory seminary "for young women in the humbler walks of life who would never get a Christian education but for a school like this."

Contrary to one of his favorite proverbs, "Don't wait for something to turn up. Go and turn up something," Dwight did not act on his dream right away.

After finishing the Boston campaign in the spring of 1877, Dwight and Sankey had shorter missions in several New England cities. They were thankful the tide had not turned against them, and they conducted several successful campaigns in places like Hartford, Connecticut, where the Hartford *Religious Herald* had positive things to say: "The wave of sympathy with them has been so strong that it seems to have flowed out and covered everything. We have come to a time when, for a season at least, Religion has come to the front."

Dwight even received an invitation to preach at Yale

University in New Haven, Connecticut; he preached to eleven hundred students for two weeks in a specially constructed building. The students were respectful and receptive to the message Dwight preached.

But the dream of a girls' school in Northfield did not disappear, and by the fall of 1878 Dwight was in Northfield discussing the school project with H. N. F. Marshall of Boston. Just then, the owner of sixteen acres adjoining Dwight's home passed by.

Dwight called to him, "Would you sell your property?"

Within minutes papers had been exchanged and signed. Soon more adjoining lots were bought, and before long a hundred acres were available for the school.

While planning for the school continued, another great event took place in the Moody family. April 11, 1879 brought the birth of Paul Dwight Moody. He was ten years younger than Dwight's son Will and thirteen and a half years younger than Emma. How Dwight rejoiced over this newest addition to his family! How good God was to him!

Four months later, on August 21, Dwight laid the cornerstone for the recitation hall, using not a proffered silver trowel, but his father's old working trowel, and Sankey sang "The Ninety and Nine." Durant gave the dedication address, emphasizing the need for such a school and its aims and ideals: "It will be a thorough school, it will be non-sectarian, and it will be Christian. Working together the Christian home, the Christian Church and this Christian school will turn out young women of the type greatly needed to do the Lord's work in the world."

They placed in the cornerstone a Bible, national and

local newspapers, two histories of Northfield, some Moody heirlooms, and a piece of the early eighteenth century Parson Doolittle's gravestone—the good Parson's grave was on the same site as the school.

Dwight decided that if Wellesley College could fix its annual fee at $250, his secondary school need require no more than $100, half the estimate for keeping and educating the students. He asked friends, acquaintances, and wealthy philanthropists for money for his project, stressing the school's threefold basis: the Bible as a vital part of the curriculum; every girl to take regular share in domestic duties whatever her home background, thus inculcating a right sense of proportion while keeping down the cost of running the school; and the low fee.

After Dwight appointed as principal a young Wellesley woman, Harriet Tuttle, the school commenced its first term despite the unfinished recitation hall. To meet the need for boarding pupils since the dormitory had not yet been built, Dwight adapted part of the coach house on his property, forming cubicles for up to twenty-five girls.

The Moodys left in the fall for the Midwest, and on November 3, the first pupils arrived during a record blizzard which laid snow sixteen inches deep. Jennie Sikes, the girl from the mountain, got the highest marks on the entrance examination.

The recitation hall remained unfinished for another month, and lessons were done in the Moodys parlor. From St. Louis, Dwight wrote continuously about the school: "Has the children got into the new school building yet?" and "How do they like it?" and "How do they like the teachers?"

Finally in the spring of 1880, Dwight could see his school taking shape. The recitation hall had been finished and the foundation laid for the first dormitory, East Hall. A hundred girls were enrolled, and Dwight ran races with them and addressed them at school prayers. The dream took shape despite setbacks.

Dwight spoke of his dream at the formal dedication of East Hall during summer vacation. After commenting, "my lack of education has always been a great disadvantage to me. I shall suffer from it as long as I live," he went on: "I hope after all of us who are here today are dead and gone this school may live and be a blessing to the world, and that missionaries may go out from here and preach the Gospel to the heathen, and it may be recognized as a power in bringing souls to Christ." He declared as the school motto a verse from Isaiah 27:3: "I the Lord do keep it; I will water it every moment: lest any hurt it, I will keep it night and day."

Last of all, Dwight prayed for the school. "The words of that prayer," said a participant from Boston, "burned into our souls." Dwight thanked God for the urge to found the school, for the friends whose gifts had raised it. Then he prayed, "O Lord, we pray that no teachers may ever come within its walls except as they have been taught by the Holy Spirit; that no scholars may ever come here except as the Spirit of God shall touch their hearts. O, God, we are Thine, this building is Thine! We give it over to Thee. Take it and keep it and bless it, with Thy keeping power!"

Ever since the girls' school had started, Dwight had felt prodded to start something for boys—either that or admit boys to the present school. Why, Dwight wondered, should he "add to his troubles?" But the demands increased. One day wealthy Hiram Camp, befriended by Dwight in his 1878 New Haven campaign, appeared in Northfield. Would Dwight help him make out his will?

"Why not be your own executor?" Dwight asked. "You've had all the work of acquiring your means; why not have the fun of seeing it do good?"

"Well, to what should I give?" queried Camp.

"What is your denomination?"

"I am a Congregationalist," Camp responded.

"Well, then, give to some one of the many societies of your church. They are well manned and it will be wisely used," suggested Dwight.

"But," protested Camp, "I wish to give to something specific; I want to see what I do."

"All right," said Dwight, "Here is the very thing. People have been after me to take boys into Northfield. I'm not going to increase my troubles that way. Then they want me to start a school for boys on the same lines as Northfield, but I want someone else to do it. Now, Mr. Camp, there is something for you to do."

The elderly Mr. Camp scarcely thought he could launch such a project, but he urged Dwight to undertake it and offered twenty-five-thousand dollars as a starter. What an awkward position this presented to Dwight! He felt he was already spread too thin. How would he finance yet another school? But he had been so convincing, he found himself with no other recourse than to start it himself!

With the money from Mr. Camp, Dwight looked for a suitable site, and finally found 275 acres five miles across the river from the girls' school (called the seminary). Ironically, the acreage belonged to Ezra Purple, the heartless mortgager who, when Dwight's father died, had demanded of the sick widow a quit-claim deed to the homestead.

Mr. Camp suggested the name Mount Hermon for the boys' school based on Psalm 135:3: "For there the Lord commanded the blessing, even life for evermore." The first boys, from eight to twelve years old, arrived on May 4, 1881. Three years later, with increasing applications from older boys and increasing troubles with the younger ones, Dwight decided to accept no applicants under sixteen. Like the seminary, the Bible was central, costs were $100 a year, and "manual labor" required of all.

Student John T. Tildsey recalled his daily stint:

"Moody was a realist. He would give each boy some touch with the working world which had been the main means of his own education. So I each day, for example, went from my Greek, Latin, or Mathematics class to my class in Pig Nurture. In this class I speedily acquired the art of tackling, which stood me in good stead on the football field."

The following year, Tildsey served as boss on the sanitary squad; after that, he was first officer of a cottage—responsible for the care of the building and for the conduct of twenty boys living in it. He finally became assistant librarian in charge of evening study in the library.

Each student was graded on the basis of his performance of this "dirty work," this grade being considered just as important an indication of character and future success as were their classroom grades.

The daily schedule from 6:00 A.M.. to 10:00 P.M. left little time for loafing, and unlike the seminary, Mount Hermon kept in session through the summer months, making three terms of four months each, partly due to the fact that the livestock and gardens needed tending all year. Within four years, with accommodations for only eighty, Dwight was besieged yearly with three hundred applications. A more cosmopolitan student body would have been hard to find. At one time, there were students from nearly every state and from thirty-two nations!

At first the school was little more than a fair grammar school. However, in 1883, after two years at Mount Hermon, two brothers announced to Dwight they were leaving for home because their mother wanted them to prepare for college.

Dwight begged them to stay, telling them: "The world has too many college men—too many men with book learning—too many smart men. The college is not turning out men needed for today. What we want is men who can go out as colporteurs, YMCA secretaries, Bible readers and city missionaries. Take a short cut through a preparatory school and get to work."

He believed and preached that education could make one only a more clever rascal! He shared with a friend that "education does not save a man. An educated rascal is the worst rascal of all. I have over 1100 students in my school, and I have often said that if I knew they were going to turn out bad I wouldn't educate them."

In keeping with his views, Dwight made a point of

notifying all applicants and their parents that Mount Hermon was no refuge for delinquents. "The school is for young men of sound bodies, good minds, and high aims. Vicious or idle boys are not wanted. It is neither a reformatory for the depraved nor an asylum for the exposed," he said on one occasion.

Gradually, as he worked increasingly with colleges and college students, Dwight's ideas changed, and Northfield began to take on more academic distinction. As long as he lived, however, his primary concern for each student was a spiritual one. He said, "I want to help the students into lives that will count for the cause of Christ."

Toward this end as each school year began, before he left for his winter season of big-city campaigning, Dwight urged the student body to become "out-and-out believers in Christ." There was no undue pressure, but Dwight wished every student to be a "wholesome, happy Christian."

Many students who could not otherwise have afforded even the very low cost of the schools were granted tuition-free scholarships, provided they met the preliminary conditions. But Dwight remained a strict disciplinarian regarding the rules set down.

With his evangelistic work and other obligations, the problem of school financing was not easy. The students helped with their manual labor to keep costs down, but still their one hundred dollars was but half the cost of providing their education, and how Dwight got the rest of the funds did not matter particularly to the resourceful educator. One afternoon, in the midst of a seminary trustees' meeting, a member left early and was about to enter his carriage when Dwight raised a window and yelled, "Will you give a thousand dollars if I will do the same?"

"All right," agreed the trustee.

Dwight closed the window, confessing he did not have the thousand dollars but would raise it "one way or another." At this, another trustee smiled and remarked that such a proceeding was, to say the least, irregular. Dwight answered, "Oh well, we do everything up here differently from other people."

Dwight was short on protocol but long on effectiveness. One day he heard that Pittsburgh's William Thaw was giving away his money. He packed his bag and went to see him, only to find a long line of people ahead of him. He learned the philanthropist was giving a maximum of three hundred dollars to each case. When it came Dwight's turn he introduced himself as, "Mr. Moody, from Northfield."

"What, the great evangelist! Well, I'm delighted to see you here."

"Perhaps," suggested Dwight, "you won't be, when you learn what I'm here for. We are trying to give poor young men a Christian education, and we have to turn away hundreds of applicants each year. I'd like you to give us $10,000 toward a building."

"But I'm not giving more than $300 to each case."

"But, this is a special case."

"Yes, I know, and I'll give $5000."

"Don't you believe in me and this work? Why not at once give the money? I can stand in line and beg $300 at a time, but I must be off and build this building."

Of course, Dwight got his money!

Increasingly Dwight resorted to letters to request funds, but he refused to use a rubber stamp of his signature, insisting on signing each one carefully, spreading them all over his room so as not to blot before they dried. With each letter he sent a little book, describing the schools, went on with a paragraph or two of his own description, and closed by noting:

I hope to live long enough to have one thousand friends, each subscribing a hundred dollars a year for the support of one student. Will you not join the list? Or if not, will you not set aside a contribution—however small—for this purpose between now and June?

A great surprise happened at "Temptation Hill," so named by Dwight that some friend might be tempted to give money enough to erect a chapel. By 1897, Dwight's sixtieth birthday, nobody had taken the hint, so F. B. Meyer and Henry Moore took matters into their own hands and raised enough money in England and America to put up a memorial chapel. Dwight, however, refused to consider it a memorial for him, and would not permit a note of this on the bronze tablet in the vestibule:

THIS CHAPEL WAS ERECTED BY CONTRIBUTIONS OF CHRISTIAN FRIENDS IN GREAT BRITAIN AND THE UNITED STATES, FOR THE GLORY OF GOD AND TO BE A PERPETUAL WITNESS TO THEIR UNITY IN THE SERVICE OF CHRIST.

Two other things Dwight refused was to raise the tuition

or to have either school endowed. By raising the tuition he felt he would defeat the very purpose for which he had ordained the schools, that of helping the underprivileged, and by endowing them, he felt they would wither.

When asked why he didn't operate his schools on faith in a fashion like George Muller of Bristol, England, Dwight replied, "I do. I always have and always will. As an evidence of it if you will tell me of any Christian man who had money to whom I have not written or on whom I have not called, I will do so at once. I show my faith when I go to men and ask them to give to God's work."

Dwight's parting words to the public regarding his beloved schools were given in New York City at the Fifth Avenue Presbyterian Church just before leaving for the Kansas City campaign:

> *You may read in the papers that Moody is dead. It will not be so. God has given me the gift of life everlasting. Five and twenty years ago in my native village of Northfield I planted two Christian schools for the training of boys and maidens in Christian living and consecration as teachers and missionaries of Jesus Christ. I bequeath as my legacy those training schools for Jesus to the churches of America, and I only ask that visitors to the beautiful native village where my ashes slumber on consecrated Round Top when they go there shall not be pained with the sight of melancholy ruins wrought by*

> *cruel neglect, but rather shall be greeted*
> *by the spectacle of two great, glorious*
> *lighthouses of the Lord, beaming out over*
> *the land, over the continent, over the*
> *world.*

Much of Dwight's original dream had already been fulfilled at the time of his death—due in no small part to his wisdom, drive, and sacrifice.

Twenty-one

Final Days

*E*ven while Dwight was occupied with building two schools in Northfield, he saw the need for a school in Chicago to train Christian laymen for the church. He had nothing against theological seminaries, stating, "They have their place." As he pointed out, "A young man doesn't know until he is twenty or twenty-three what he wants to do for a profession. But if he waits till then to decide to be a minister and goes to college or seminary, he will be fifty years old by the time he is ready to begin work."

Dwight was interested in helping college and seminary graduates, ministers and missionaries, and laymen who were interested in pursuing English Bible study and practical evangelism. With the latter group he wanted to reach "the three-fourths that do not go anywhere to church," thus getting "a lever under all the churches." He wanted men and women who were willing to "lay their lives alongside the laboring-class and the poor, and bring the gospel to bear upon their lives." He spoke from his own background working with Chicago's poor and needy.

Instrumental in the planning was Emeline Dryer, who resigned in 1873 as head of the faculty at Illinois State Normal School to go to work for Dwight in Chicago. By

1883, with Dwight again in England, her Bible classes were drawing more people than ever.

When Charles A. Blanchard, a teacher at nearby Wheaton College, asked her what her plans were, she told him of Dwight's calling her from public school work to organize just such a training school. She needed, she told Blanchard, five hundred dollars to enlarge the operations. Blanchard got involved at that time and raised the necessary money.

By the fall of 1883, Dryer had gotten Dr. William G. Moorehead of Xenia, Ohio, involved and was teaching fifty young men and women.

The previous summer, Dwight had stressed the need for city missionaries in Chicago: "I know the need of this. I walked the streets of Chicago day after day, feeling that I must preach, yet knowing that I was not fitted for the work and wanted to learn. Had there been some place where I could have been trained and allowed to study, while I was at work, I could have been more successful."

Preachers also needed more than textbook learning; they needed to be "trained in the school of human nature." As Dwight explained, "They need to rub up against the world and learn how to read men. They fail to get hold of men for this very reason."

When a New Yorker pressed Dwight to take five thousand dollars for just such a school, he felt he could not turn it down. Coming to Chicago a short time later, another five thousand dollars was given him to start the school in Chicago.

Dwight returned to the British Isles in 1883, and while he was gone, Miss Dryer met with several others each

Saturday morning to pray for guidance and support. She prayed that Dwight would "come and plan something commensurate with the needs." By January 1885, Dwight agreed to come and begin such a work if others would raise the money. But people who could do the fund-raising were busy with other ventures.

The following January, Dwight made a public appeal for funds. He told his audience that $100,000 had been raised for a building in Edinburgh, and challenged them to raise $250,000.

Every time Dwight tried to forget about the Bible Institute, he would be persuaded otherwise. Finally, he started a subscription paper. Several people sitting on the platform of his current campaign subscribed five thousand dollars apiece. Cyrus Hall McCormick offered fifty thousand dollars. Dwight suggested, "Better make it a hundred." And McCormick, tickled at Dwight's boldness, said, "That will require some consideration," but nevertheless came through with the one hundred thousand dollars.

The money seemed to pour in from everywhere for the Institute. In the meantime, training took place at the Chicago Avenue Church to provide workers for the mass evangelism Dwight had encouraged in the city. He gave the first one hundred dollars toward a large gospel tent to be pitched in "Little Hell," to be manned by an evangelist and a corps of assistants. In the winter, the mission moved into churches, missions, theaters, and even barrooms where beer kegs became seats.

Through a series of brief "Bible Institutes," training was given these workers in the Scriptures and in "practical methods of Christian work." By May, 1889, over two hundred people were attending these institutes. Dwight wrote to Whittle on May 24, telling him, "I have never been so hopeful about anything I have undertaken." He said he felt he was trying to solve "the great problem of the century."

Back in Chicago, Dwight became aware of three large houses for sale next to the Chicago Avenue Church. He bought them on the spot for three future dormitories to house fifty women seeking admission to the institute. Immediately, he began work on a three-story brick building for the ninety men who were attending as well. And on September 26, 1889, Dwight opened the institute officially, putting Reuben Torrey, a minister formerly from New Haven, Connecticut, in charge. Dwight had selected the other necessary officials at that time, so everything was in place for the institute to grow and flourish.

The daily schedule was full, and Mondays were kept for "Rest Day." In addition to "domestic" work, practical work assignments in the city were mandatory. Each week students were responsible for such tasks as organizing and carrying on cottage prayer meetings, working in a city mission or industrial school, holding children's meetings, or otherwise supplementing the work of the city churches. In typical Moody style, inquiry meetings became the rule after virtually every service.

By 1890 the men's building was finished and Dwight, surveying it, exclaimed, "There is my life work!" By fall he must have been more convinced than ever when 248 students enrolled. That year, in addition to their study, they conducted over three thousand meetings, paid ten thousand visits to homes of the poor, and went to more than one thousand saloons. By the end of the year Dwight rejoiced to see his first graduates being placed at home and abroad. Three went to India, eight to China, seven to Africa, two to South America, six to Turkey, and one each to Bulgaria, Persia, Burma, and Japan.

Forty-six of the graduates remained in the States, going into evangelistic work; thirty-one went into pastoral work; five into Sunday school missions; two into home missions; seven into YMCA work; two into YWCA work; and six into "singing evangelism." A number took posts in charitable institutions; twenty went out as teachers; and twenty-nine went on to further education. Henry Drummond had the last word on the fledgling Bible Institute saying, "It will be allowed that this is a pretty fair record for a two years' old institute." Dwight also felt pleased, and added, "My school work will not tell much until the century closes, but when I am gone I shall leave some grand men and women behind."

The instructors were always chosen carefully and had to view the Bible as literal. Dwight gave them much academic freedom but admonished them about their biblical views: "Let us take our stand here, that any man can teach upon our platforms with absolute freedom whatever he finds in the Bible, but no man shall be allowed to pick the Bible to pieces."

Dwight's students highly respected him, even revered him. When he visited Chicago, he stayed in the men's dorm and ate with them in the dining hall. Each Monday morning that Dwight was away, Torrey would write a letter to him including a statistical report for the previous week. Dwight was eager for optimistic statistics, but was even more concerned about each individual student. He held high standards and expected each of them to do the same. He wrote Torrey: "If any of the men do not come up to the mark, you will not keep them. That I told them when I left. Keep me posted about them, and give them a good trial." For all his good humor, Dwight expected every person to do his best.

One man, Charles Stetzle, had applied to seminary after seminary but was refused admission because of academic standing. At last hearing of Dwight's institute, he wrote him, giving a mutual friend as a reference. When Dwight met the friend later, he asked but one question of the applicant, "Has he sand?" By this he meant, "Has he the ability and interest necessary to acquire the training, and the consecration required for success?"

To another student who seemed to lack interest, Dwight gave the following volatile advice: "You know, I'd like to fasten about a quarter of a pound of gun-powder to the tail of your coat and set fire to it!" The student apparently took the hint and later became a city missionary in London.

Dwight implemented the Northfield plan for fundraising at the institute. He wrote potential donors, asking for $150 to support one student. He and his wife each took one student, and he went out looking for two hundred more donors.

At the end of a decade or so, Dwight's institute was more than a mere "whistling in the woods," as he himself termed it shortly before his death. More than three thousand students had enrolled, tuition free, in buildings by then worth a third of a million dollars. About a third of the alumni had gone into Christian service full-time, while most of the rest filled valuable lay positions in churches across the country. The Moody Bible Institute, as it became at his death, was now, according to the public relations department, the "West Point of Christian Work."

In addition to getting the Northfield Schools and the Bible Institute underway, the 1880s proved to be fruitful years for Dwight. He continued to receive many invitations to revisit Scotland and England. One invitation stretched 150 yards long and was signed by numerous ministers and laymen from the United Kingdom. Finally, in September 1881, the Moodys and the Sankeys set sail for the countries of their early success.

Once again crowds thronged to hear Dwight in Edinburgh, London, and even at Cambridge University. He campaigned in most of the same places he had on the earlier trip. He was less a sensation this time and more the beloved Yankee who discovered a welcome spelled out in enormous crowds, eager to hear once again the homely aphorisms, the pungent epigrams, the down-to-earth applications, and the resurrection of Bible characters in a language that was at once simple and pithy, straight forward and humorous. In some respects this second great mission was a continuation of the first; in some respects, it was a duplication.

In 1884, Dwight spoke at Cambridge University. All had been prepared: a large choir, daily prayer meetings, and extensive advertising. But the 1,700 students did not cooperate, and on opening night, were irreverent, noisy, and disruptive, even throwing a firecracker against a window. Dwight was aghast! He had preached to all kinds of people, but never had had to put up with such behavior. Sankey began to sing "The Ninety and Nine," but the men cheered, jeered, and called for an encore. Unfortunately, Dwight's subject was "Dan'l," the pronunciation of which set the students off even more.

Somehow Dwight and Sankey got through the night with increasingly heavy hearts. But a bedridden lady began to hold prayer meetings for the students, and the tide was turned. Increasingly, the students responded to the call to come to Christ, and by the end of the campaign, Dwight experienced a great victory in place of defeat.

All together, Dwight traveled to the British Isles seven times. The first three trips helped him to set his sights. The fourth established him as front-page news in secular and religious papers alike. The fifth, sixth, and seventh trips helped consolidate and extend the work of the fourth. When he returned to America in 1892, this time to stay, he left behind a grateful people. In 1874 he had declared in England, "If America is true to herself, she will occupy a foremost place in the evangelization of the world." That she did so in the evangelization of the United Kingdom was due, in large part, to the determination of the preacher himself.

twenty-two

The Legacy

"Some day," Dwight was fond of saying, "you will read in the papers that D. L. Moody of East Northfield is dead. Don't believe a word of it! At that moment I shall be more alive than I am now!" He would then describe heaven with such conviction that fully a million people, by some estimates, forsook the paths of sin to follow Moody's Christ. Again, Dwight belonged not alone to East Northfield—the world had become his home. With his passing, millions mourned as though he belonged to their community, to their church, to their home.

He died as he lived—winning souls—for his supreme aim had become the conversion of as many souls as one man, bent on complete consecration, could muster for the heavenly roll call. It was this passion that drove him on to pace his workers as a fox paces the pursuing hounds, that drove him on when others dropped in their tracks from exhaustion, that drove him on to Kansas City, Missouri, complete with a grueling itinerary. He had promised them he would begin a campaign on November 12, 1899.

Dwight cried out to God for precious souls: "If only it would please God to let me get hold of this city by a winter of meetings! I should like to do it before I die," he confided to a friend before leaving.

As he stepped from the train in Kansas City on Saturday, November 11, the old throbbing in his chest had begun again. But he retained the old vigor, the same cheerfulness. The first night he preached on "Whatsoever a man soweth, that shall he reap." The audience hung on his every word, and many responded at the close of the message.

Dwight did not sleep that night, and his doctor insisted he quit speaking. True to form, Dwight would not quit the evening services, but he did stop the afternoon sessions. However, by afternoon he was worse, and finally he had to tell the committee that he would have to give up the meetings: "It's the first time in forty years of preaching that I have had to give up my meetings."

His associates rented a special railroad car, "The Messenger of Peace," and put Dwight aboard for the trip to Northfield. The train engineer had been converted under Dwight's ministry fifteen years before and did his utmost in speeding up the train to catch its eastern connection.

In Northfield again, Dwight rallied for a few days, and his old optimism returned. He still had plenty of work to do, "If God will grant me more days."

On the evening of December 21, lying on his bed at Northfield, Dwight wrote in pencil in his usual bold hand, "To see his star is good, but to see his face is better."

As the next dawn broke, Friday, December 22, 1899, Dwight stirred from an hour's deep sleep that had ended a fitful night of increasing weakness.

Suddenly his son Will heard in slow measured words:

"Earth recedes, heaven opens before me!" Will hurried across to him.

"No, this is no dream, Will. It is beautiful. It is like a trance. If this is death, it is sweet. God is calling me and I must go. Don't call me back!"

Just then, Emma Moody entered the room, and Dwight told her, "Mama, you have been a good dear wife." He slipped into unconsciousness, murmuring, "No pain, no valley, it's bliss."

After an injection by the doctor, he regained momentary consciousness and said he would like to get out of bed and cross over to a chair. He rose, walked to his chair almost unaided, and sat a few moments, then asked to be helped back to bed.

Nothing need keep him. His work was finished, and the chariot of God had come for him. Dwight L. Moody breathed his last and then gazed upon the face of the One whose love had given his life meaning.

HEROES OF THE FAITH

This exciting biographical series explores the lives of famous Christian men and women throughout the ages. These trade paper books will inspire and encourage you to follow the example of these "Heroes of the Faith" who made Christ the center of their existence. 208 pages each. Only $3.97 each!